Hoots!
An Anthology of Scottish
Comic Writing

Hoots!
An Anthology of Scottish Comic Writing

Edited by
Susie Maguire and David Jackson Young

Polygon
Edinburgh

© Editorial arrangements Polygon 1997
© Introduction The Editors
Pages 166-167 constitute a continuation of copyright.
Reprinted 1998

Published by
Polygon
22 George Square
Edinburgh
EH8 9LF

Set in Meridien by Palimpsest Book Production Limited,
Polmont, Stirlingshire
Printed and bound in Great Britain by
The Cromwell Press, Trowbridge, Wilts

A CIP record is available for this title

ISBN 0 7486 6229 4

The Publisher acknowledges subsidy from

THE SCOTTISH ARTS COUNCIL

towards the publication of this volume.

Contents

Introduction *The Editors*	vii
Rab's First Rant *Ian Pattison*	1
Blue Rubber Pants *Ivor Cutler*	3
The Ancient Town of Leith *William McGonagall*	4
Congress with Poets *Patricia Hannah*	7
Something to be Proud Of *James Meek*	13
The Tattoo Reviewed *Anthony Troon*	17
Christmas on the Croft with Angus Dreichmore *Neil MacVicar*	19
A Ministerial Debut *John Galt*	22
Going Messages For Mistress Munro *Lewis Grassic Gibbon*	25
Scott's Porrij *Alison Kermack*	29
Stone-Age Sheep *David Deans*	30
'There was a young fellow named Weir...' *Anon*	33
The Trendelenburg Position *Alasdair Gray*	34
Alba Einstein *Robert Crawford*	41
Spaced Out *David Crooks*	42
Glasgow Song *Forbes Masson and Alan Cumming*	49
The Wee Cock Sparra *Hugh Frater and Duncan Macrae*	52
The Night Class *Arnold Brown*	54
The Story of Major Cartwright, by Murdo *Iain Crichton Smith*	59
Proposal *Doreen Watson*	63
Scene From a Marriage *Susan Ferrier*	64
The Scot's Lament *Will Fyffe*	71
Linoleum *Neil Munro*	72
Brief Encounter *Harry Ritchie*	77

1964: Holiday! *Kate Atkinson*	79
A Hole in One *Ludovic Kennedy*	85
Cutting a Dash *Muriel Gray*	86
'There was an Old Man of the Cape . . .' *R.L. Stevenson*	92
Supper Isna Ready *Anon*	93
Allergy *Elspeth Davie*	94
A Tale of Ordinary Love *David Kilby*	102
The Natural History of Scotland *John McKay*	108
A Burial at Sea *Eric Linklater*	110
Tweed Versus Till *Anon*	115
Sally Simpkin's Lament *Thomas Hood*	116
Barry Norman's Tie *Susie Maguire*	118
Favourite Shade *Liz Lochhead*	126
Changing a Downie Cover *Angela McSeveney*	128
The Mummy *Edwin Morgan*	129
In the Dock: Irvine Welsh *Raymond Travers*	132
Where the Debris Meets the Sea *Irvine Welsh*	135
A Literary Football Match *Leonard Maguire*	142
The Ways and Wiles o' Oor Wullie *Anon*	145
Cover Story *James Cameron*	146
Why the Elgin Marbles Must Be Returned to Elgin *W.N. Herbert*	149
Sympathy for the De'il *James Robertson*	151
Wee Jaikie's Sang *Donald Gordon*	156
Bodily Functions *Tom Morton*	157
Scotland *Alastair Reid*	163
Postscript *James Sinclair*	164
Notes on Editors	165
Copyright acknowledgements	166

The Editors

Introduction

'Get in. Get out. Don't linger.'

Raymond Carver's typically terse advice to the aspiring short story writer is equally applicable to the aspiring writer of introductions. Indeed, since most people never read introductions, and those few who do usually come to them having already got through at least two-thirds of the rest of the book, there's a good argument for dispensing with them altogether – or for using the space for some other purpose, such as saying 'hello' to one's friends in print.

But on the assumption that you're perusing these opening pages in the innocent and genuine expectation of actually being introduced to what follows, let's get straight to the point.

Beware. What follows has about as much to do with our exclamatory, monosyllabic title as the small print of a mortgage advertisement has to do with those attention-grabbing interest rates they quote at the top of the page. *'Hoots!'* and '4½%!'. Both are designed to pull you in by the lapels. And just as the latter may lead you to expect improbably low monthly payments (which they won't be), so the former might perhaps suggest some sort of red-nosed tartan joke book (which this isn't). As for our marginally less hysterical subtitle – *An Anthology of Scottish Comic Writing* – well, that's almost as misleading, insofar as the most important word in the phrase is probably the first one.

The Editors

Because this is very much *an* anthology, a personal selection of comic writing which happens to be by Scottish authors. In no sense is it designed to be *the* definitive bringing-together of the finest Caledonian humour from the first Pictish one-liner to the present day, and readers expecting a comprehensive collection that spans the centuries are advised to look elsewhere.

Apart from the fact that all the material included in these pages meets our own comic criteria (i.e., it makes us laugh), what most of our selections have in common is the fact that you almost certainly won't find them in any of the other English-language humour anthologies already in the bookshops. For some reason the editors of these books seem reluctant to cast their literary nets much north of Watford (or much north of Hampstead, for that matter); and so in a bold gesture of positive discrimination, Polygon have asked us – with a handful of exceptions – to cast our own nets no further south than the Carter Bar.

So: what characteristics, if any, do these pieces of Scottish comic writing share, beyond their geographical origin? Does such a thing emerge as a distinctly Scottish sense of humour? In the interests of not lingering, we'll leave it to the reviewers – and readers with time on their hands – to answer these questions (although Sydney Smith and Ludovic Kennedy have a stab at it on page 85).

For what it's worth, though, our guess is that you'd be hard pushed to find much of a connection between Tom Morton's scatological misadventures and Patricia Hannah's elegant literary satire; or between David Kilby's painfully funny funeral oration, and the surrealistic ramblings of Ivor Cutler. In other words, all human life is here, and variety is the spice of it.

When I'm not writing introductions I work for BBC Radio, and quite a number of the pieces included in this

Introduction

book were first presented to the public in Radio Scotland's *Storyline* and Radio 4's *Short Story*, produced by me or by one of my colleagues in Edinburgh. This book is, in part, a belated response to those listeners who over the years were sufficiently amused by what they heard to write in and ask where the material could be found in print.

A lot of our selections, therefore – particularly the short stories – are by new and largely unknown writers. We hope you'll enjoy discovering them (or, if you caught them on the radio, seeing their work on the page). But by way of providing what broadcasting executives call 'entry points' in our 'schedule', we've also included a liberal sprinkling of familiar names – though, like Lewis Grassic Gibbon, for example, they're not always names that you'd immediately associate with comic writing. Or if they are known for their humour, we've tried to represent them by a less familiar piece of work, hence the inclusion of one of Neil Munro's *Jimmy Swan* stories, rather than a *Para Handy* tale.

Finally, please note that there is no special significance in the disproportionate number of quotations from the late, great Chic Murray scattered through these pages, beyond the fact that we both just find him particularly funny. And although, unlike most of the material in this book, his jokes were written primarily for performance, it's impossible to read them without hearing Murray's inimitably droll delivery.

There was a man who got in, got out, and *did* linger – most effectively.

David Jackson Young
February 1997

Yes indeedy.

Susie Maguire
February 1997

The Editors

Thanks . . .

Thanks to all those who suggested items for inclusion in this anthology – whether or not these were finally incorporated! And particular thanks to Marion Sinclair at Polygon for her support in getting the book off the ground, through the presses, and on to the shelves.

S.M. and D.J.Y.

Editors' Mission Statement

'I got up this morning. I like to get up in the morning; it gives me the rest of the day to myself.'

Chic Murray
(1919–1985)

Ian Pattison (b. 1950)

Rab's First Rant

A nondescript Glasgow street by night, the darkness lit by yellow sodium street lamps. The camera tracks a disreputable looking passer-by as he walks along. He wears a shiny, stained blue suit, with a string vest visible directly under the jacket. There's a soiled white bandage round his head. When first responding to the off-camera interviewer he looks furtive and evasive, but becomes more and more expressive as he warms to his theme, jabbing the air with a tightly rolled-up newspaper to emphasise a point. This is Rab C. Nesbitt's television debut . . .

Are you talking to me?
 Don't you talk to me – away ye . . .
 Listen, I'll tell ye. The trouble with this Tory government, is what they're daein' to people – to people like me, and there ye are. See people like them? See people like me? It's OTT a'thigither. There.
 An' – an' – an' I mean, ye can talk aboot yer Thirties! Yer Thirties, eh? Christ, I lived – I *lived* through the Thirties. I had TB! I had ringworm! I saw *The Jazz Singer* four times – Christ, I know what I'm talkin' aboot!
 I mean, ye can talk aboot yer Holocaust, eh? That's fair enough, yer Holocaust. But Christ, that was a – that was a *skive* compared to this, that was a *doddle* compared to this. I mean have you tried gettin' a sick line efter five days, eh? Eh? No. Away ye . . . Christ, don't you talk to me.
 And the worst o' it is, ye can see the buggers, see them sittin' there. Sittin' there oan the telly in their

1

Ian Pattison

dinner-jackets. In their *dinner-jackets*. Sittin there. Havin' their dinners. Wi' their *yah-de-dah* this, an' their *lah-de-dah* that. An' see when it – see when it comes doon tae it, they're nae better than I am. They're nae better than I am! In fact, they're *worse* than I am. There ye are, they're worse than I am. An' I'm scum! I mean, what does that make them, eh?

I mean maybe you can work it oot because I cannae. But then again, who am I, eh? Who am I? Eh? Nah, nah. See when ye, see when ye scrape it a' away, a' the crap, an' ye get right doon tae it, I mean right doon tae the bottom line, they're a' a lot o' jumped-up fascist bastards, *that's* what they are!

I'll tell ye something else, son, I should know, for I was an inspector in the buses. There ye are.

But I mean what is the answer? Eh? Maybe you can tell me what the answer is, because I'm *Donald Ducked* if *I* know what the answer is.

What was yer question again?

Ivor Cutler   (b. 1923)

Blue Rubber Pants

One morning, Mother fastened a fresh nappy on to me, pulled a pair of blue rubber pants over it and sat me in the cot. The rubber smell was new and exciting.

My hands sought out the hemless edge. To my delight, the rubber tore, soft and quiet. A deep satisfied peace entered me.

I sought out new areas to tear and, after a short space, the pants were in ribbons and I was a very happy boy.

When Mother came in to see me, she gave a cry of amused exasperation, fetched a second pair and fastened them on, removing the tatters.

'Oh, thank you,' I thought and went to work. The performance was repeated, minus Mother's amusement.

The third pair was torn in a perfunctory way. Sensual saturation having been reached, my heart was no longer in it, like an executioner having chopped off his hundredth head.

Mother entered the room, froze, her face bright red, and began to shout at me. It was my first crit. I was not being understood. I shall die not being understood, like the rest of you.

(from GLASGOW DREAMER)

William McGonagall (?1825–1902)

The Ancient Town of Leith

Ancient town of Leith, most wonderful to be seen,
With your many handsome buildings, and lovely links so green,
And the first buildings I may mention are the Courthouse and Town Hall,
Also Trinity House, and the Sailors' Home of Call.

Then as for Leith Fort, it was erected in 1779, which is really grand,
And which is now the artillery headquarters in Bonnie Scotland;
And as for the Docks, they are magnificent to see,
They comprise five docks, two piers, 1,141 yards long respectively.

And there's steam boat communication with London and the North of Scotland,
And the fares are really cheap and the accommodation most grand;
Then there's many public works in Leith, such as flour mills,
And chemical works, where medicines are made for curing many ills.

Besides, there are sugar refineries and distilleries,
Also engineer works, saw-mills, rope-works, and breweries,

The Ancient Town of Leith

Where many of the inhabitants are daily employed,
And the wages they receive make their hearts feel overjoyed.

In past times Leith shared the fortunes of Edinboro',
Because it withstood nine months' siege, which caused them great sorrow;
They fought against the Protestants in 1559 and in '60,
But they beat them back manfully and made them flee.
Then there's Bailie Gibson's fish shop, most elegant to be seen,
And the fish he sells there are beautiful and clean;
And for himself, he is a very good man,
And to deny it there's few people can.

The suburban villas of Leith are elegant and grand,
With accommodation that might suit the greatest lady in the land;
And the air is pure and good for the people's health,—
And health, I'm sure, is better by far than wealth.

The Links of Leith are beautiful for golfers to play,
After they have finished the toils of the day;
It is good for their health to play at golf there,
On that very beautiful green, and breathe the pure air.

The old town of Leith is situated at the junction of the River of Leith,
Which springs from the land of heather and heath;
And no part in the Empire is growing so rapidly,
Which the inhabitants of Leith are right glad to see.

And Leith in every way is in itself independent,
And has been too busy to attend to its own adornment;
But I venture to say and also mention
That the authorities to the town will pay more attention.

William McGonagall

Ancient town of Leith, I must now conclude my muse,
And to write in praise of thee my pen does not refuse,
Because the inhabitants to me have been very kind,
And I'm sure more generous people would be hard
   to find.

They are very affable in temper and void of pride,
And I hope God will always for them provide;
May He shower His blessings upon them by land
   and sea,
Because they have always been very kind to me.

* * *

'When the wife of an artist, painter, singer or whatnot, goes about saying she "doesn't understand anything about her husband's particular art", you may be sure that he is not very good in his line. Many women have no understanding of the arts, but all women know talent when they share a bed with it.'
Catherine Carswell
(1879–1946)

Patricia Hannah (b. 1945)

Congress with Poets

Philip Larkin isn't dead; I know this for a fact. Well, Philip Larkin the *poet* is dead, to all extents and purposes, because now he calls himself Alec Macintosh, Captain RN (retired), and lives next door to me. Captain Macintosh will only say he was in submarines; any more questions and he lights his pipe and quotes the Official Secrets Act. But it's Philip Larkin all right, I recognised him at once; and who else would choose a past in a submarine when the world was his oyster?

There are a lot of retired people in our street; professional people, doctors and university lecturers and a few military types. Philip Larkin is our only Naval man, which is nice for him – no awkward questions about Pompey and Chicken on a Raft and that sort of thing, although I suppose he could excuse his ignorance by saying he was underneath the polar ice cap at the time. That would be a very Philip Larkin sort of thing: upping periscope in the frozen north when everyone else was having fun. It would also explain why he missed all the sex – though I can't say I noticed it much myself and I have been on dry land all my life, except for the Caledonian MacBrayne ferry to Mull.

Our street is a street of big Victorian houses; Scottish Baronial romances, converted now into flats, and the gardens divided up into plots big enough to potter in without the use of those noisy power tools. Gardening used to be peaceful, but as no one works in dark satanic mills any more they feel the need to recreate them in their

Patricia Hannah

gardens at the weekend: man and machine toiling in a nightmare of hot oil and noise to hack a two foot privet hedge from the green hell of a suburban garden. There's nothing of that sort of thing here; we cultivate the lost art of good manners. From time to time a voice, developed by a lifetime in command, will boom out instructions to dogs or women, and occasionally the sound of a sherry party will drift through open windows on a summer evening, but nothing unpleasant. The minister at number nine sometimes has people in for Bible Study and prayers. He's evangelically inclined, and by the time they leave in the wee small hours they're chock-a-block with the Holy Ghost – no speaking in tongues, thank goodness, just a lot of 'Cheerie-byes' and Jesus Saves tooted on car horns. Otherwise, it really is quiet; even the murder at number seven was a poisoning so no one heard a thing.

It's not that we aren't aware of social problems; we all watch the six o' clock news, and one house in the street was bought last year by what Professor Black at number five calls the Nouveau Posh. They had the interior decorators in so the windows are swagged with triple-pleated drapes and festoon blinds in Sanderson's Grange and Laura Ashley fabrics. In the back garden they have white cast-plastic Heritage furniture and a barbecue on wheels that looks disconcertingly like a pram – it's quite unpleasant to see him poking about under the hood with a large toasting fork. The front garden boasts his Volvo, a pink Japanese flowering cherry and a white Japanese jeep with a cowcatcher bolted to the front in case the wife should encounter a herd of bison or an Edinburgh rock fall on her way to Marks and Spencer. There was a bit of trouble early on with the children, but they've been sent to Gordonstoun; and the curtains will fade with time.

Philip Larkin isn't at all like that; he's pleasant and polite – always says good-morning and tips his cap to ladies; and you don't see much of that nowadays. His garden's at the back like mine, I can see it from my window; but where I've gone for the bosky woodland glade effect, his garden is shipshape, laid out in straight lines – path up the middle; lawn to the right; flowers to the left, each plant a regulation twelve inches from its neighbour. The path leads to a small greenhouse with four tomato plants, tins of weed killer and pesticides in straight rows, and the wellington boots standing side by side at the door, his and his wife's, a regulation twelve inches apart.

Oh yes, he's married now, to a small brisk lady with short grey hair and Black Watch tartan slacks. They wear matching waterproof jackets and are very happy. I see them most days, loading their golf clubs into the back of the car and laughing. Philip Larkin has taken up golf, and it's done him the world of good.

You can understand why he did it, died that is: all these years in Hull with no one to talk to except other librarians and poets – no wonder he read Playboy in the lav and had a somewhat jaundiced view of the world. Then he met Marjory and his whole life changed. Or did he first decide to get out, and met Marjory afterwards? Whichever it was, he's not writing poetry any more.

Now, I haven't marched up to him in the street and said, 'You're Philip Larkin!' And he's said, 'Yes, but keep it quiet, and by the way, I don't write poetry any more.' We're great respecters of privacy round here. No, how I know about the poetry is because Marjory looks so well; all weather-beaten and striding about in her brogues with a mashie-niblick over her shoulder. She'd be dead or dying by now if he were still a poet.

Have you noticed that, how poets kill their wives? A poet marries a bookish young girl and within five years she's a nervous wreck and then dead. Six months after the funeral he publishes his latest slim volume called *A Cold Birthing* or *Wild Geese Over Lochmaben* (much acclaimed for its honest sensitivity), and then he's off to find another bookish girl.

There must be dozens of them, poets that is, hanging about outside Humanities departments, their hands deep in the pockets of their corduroy jackets, gloomily kicking tin cans along the gutters and sighing; waiting for foolish virgins. It really is something student welfare departments, or whatever they call themselves nowadays, should mention in their handbooks: 'Girls, avoid congress with poets.' They could put it in the section dealing with Safe Sex, because statistics will show that sex with a poet spells curtains for nice girls. No sooner has Charlotte or Caroline smiled at one of them than he's telling her about his strophes and antistrophes and the sunset shining on wee lochans, and all the time he's thinking what a great poem he'll write about his pain when she's put her head in the gas oven or fallen out the bathroom window, leaving a long pink rivulet of Windowlene all down the pebbledash.

Very few women survive the strain of being a White Goddess *and* a Good Cook. I grant you Mrs Thomas lived to dance on her poet's grave, but she was Welsh, and growing up to the sound of male voice choirs in the hillside probably made her unusually resilient. I myself was once chased round a table by a major Scottish poet; but I was too young, seventeen, and thought him a dirty old man. A few years later and I might have found his breathless endearments quite enchanting. He's dead now, but not before he got through two wives and a mistress.

Whatever his failings, you didn't hear of Philip Larkin lurking outside lectures on the Romantic poets, waiting to snare some girl with her head full of Shelley. He sat quietly at home on his G-plan studio couch, writing postcards to Kingsley Amis and waiting for the kettle to boil while some cool jazz brooded in the background.

Oh, there must have been girls – why else do men

Congress with Poets

become poets if not in the hope that some of the glamour of Burns and Byron will rub off on them. My friend Susan went out with a poet at university (I'm going back a few years now) because he looked like Louis MacNeice; but she caught him at home one afternoon wearing a hairnet, and once she'd seen the groove made by the elastic round the edge of his smooth black hairline she couldn't not see it, and that was that.

Hair's important to poets – their Samson's heel so to speak. Burns caught his death of cold immersing himself in the Solway Firth in a futile attempt to prevent further hair loss – you can see it's receding in the Nasmyth portrait; his hair, not the Solway Firth. Would Clarinda have wasted even one tuppenny stamp on a bald Burns? *'Though a' the locks fa' frae ma pate, Ye'll loo me yet, ma bonnie mate.'* Oh no, she'd have closed the lid of her escritoire and curled up by the fire with a glass of claret and sweet golden fingers of Helensburgh Tablet. Roaring boys need a good head of hair.

But being middle-aged was Philip Larkin's forte; even without epic hair there must have been girls who thought, 'Wow, Philip Larkin!' and one by one, over the years, sat on his studio couch, their feet together, their hands folded in their laps, waiting for the idyll. Then he'd said the three words every girl dreads to hear from a man; he'd said, 'Listen to this', and one by one they'd listened for hours till Dizzie Gillespie and Miles Davis had blown the look of radiant anticipation off each face. At least with *Tristan and Isolde* or the *Sounds of Famous Steam Engines* one can daydream – jazz doesn't allow that; it doesn't allow you to go anywhere.

So the poor girls sat, aching with boredom and observing Philip Larkin's prosaic hairdo, until he went to make coffee and they could find their coats and handbags and tiptoe away into the night.

Did he ever wonder where they'd gone?

Patricia Hannah

Humming along to Acker Bilk or whatever, and gently lifting his eggs from the bubbling water into the egg cups, Philip Larkin was happy to be alone – he'd sent ever so many postcards saying so.

I can imagine it, the moment he saw his life in all its bleakness, and something inside him snapped ... He's carried the tray with his pot of tea and boiled eggs and toast into the dining room; the rain's slanting across the soot-streaked window and the gas fire's popping and hissing, and he looks at the table with its brown Feltico heatproof cover and the tea cloth folded across one end, and he says 'Sod this' and goes off to find Marjory and a nice flat near the Golf Club.

That's another thing he doesn't do any more – listen to jazz.

Yes, I know there must have been a body; but take any man in his sixties, dead, prop him up in bed in a raincoat and horn-rimmed glasses, put bicycle clips in one hand and a secret diary in the other and who's to know the difference? Quick! What does Philip Larkin look like? ... Exactly.

Well, I can look out my window right now – I have an attic flat and a good view of most of the gardens – and there's Philip Larkin and Marjory, knocking balls round the mini putting course he's laid out on the lawn. She's breaking in her new golf shoes before the Craigielee Senior Ladies' Championship on Saturday, but he's wearing his old carpet slippers – and why not, if he's comfortable?

James Meek   (b. 1962)

Something to be Proud Of

In Edinburgh an American looked up at the castle, if it was the castle and not a housing project. He saw a crowd of citizens and tourists beginning to gather against the railings on the other side of Princes Street. He crossed the road and looked down into the park. Nothing exciting was happening.

After a time a tremor ran through the crowd and he followed their eyes up to the castle battlements. A row of figures appeared. They were standing on the very edge of the wall. There were ten of them. It was hard to make out details at such a distance, but their bodies were unnaturally bulky. He turned to the man standing on his left.

Is there going to be some kind of display? he asked. The man glared at him.

I suppose you think we all wear kilts? he said. Fucking Americans. Fucking tourists. I suppose you think we're all really quaint? I suppose you think the fucking royal family's really great?

I didn't mean to be rude, said the American.

If there's one thing worse than fucking Americans . . . hang on, I don't mean that. Right. If there's one thing worse than bloody Americans, it's the bloody English. He raised his finger into the American's face. I remember the Prince over the water. Bloody English chopped his head off. After we beat them at Culloden. They made the Highlanders walk home. Without a pension too. What a way to treat the inventors of the postage stamp, eh? Makes you think. And thae Americans. We give them their independence and what do they give us? Bloody missiles. And us the inventors of the television set. God, if John Knox was alive today, there'd be none of these pape's missiles stirring up hatred and dissension. And John Maclean! What a man! Dead like the rest of them. And him the inventor of toothpaste. Oh flower of Scotland we'll never see your like again, no, no, no. Och but the people need a leader. Man from the tenements. Up the close, out the yard, down from the hills. Like Robespierre. Or Lenin. He was Scottish. I was at school with him. I was. Aye! Aye.

I'm sorry, I can't understand a word you're saying, said the American. He turned away and lifted up his camera, which had a powerful zoom lens, and looked through it at the figures on the ramparts.

It was a line of men in camouflage uniforms. They were standing to attention, about ten feet apart, their faces hard and expressionless. They were big men. They wore khaki berets and each had a pair of green canvas wings strapped to his arms. As the American watched, the figure on the far right appeared to shout something. The ten opened their wings in unison, held them stretched, then lowered them again. The crowd got very excited.

Standing erect and aloof near the American, with his hands behind his back, was a tall, middle-aged man wearing a tweed jacket and a kilt. He had a silver moustache, a striped tie and a Rotary Club badge on his lapel. He turned and spoke to the American.

Should be a good display, he said.

Oh, it is a display, then.

Aerobatics! said the man.

I've just arrived, said the American. Who's going to be flying?

Something to be Proud Of

It's my old regiment, the Clackmannans. Battle honours go back to the first Afghan campaign.

You flew with them?

We don't call it flying in the army, said the man. We say 'winging it'.

I see.

Or 'doing the grouse'.

Right.

Or 'walking Johnny cloud'. Yes, I was an officer in the Fifties. Saw action in Suez.

My cousin was in the air force, said the American.

Aeroplanes have a place, I suppose, said the old officer. I never had much truck with the things myself.

Are these just ordinary soldiers?

This is our crack team! The Red Dragons. Not often you see a soldier's arms in canvas these days. Things aren't what they were. Clackmannans had fourteen battalions on the Somme. Like starlings.

So what do you reckon they'll do in this display?

Well, said the old officer, gesturing with his hands, I should think they'll start out with a couple of circuits of the castle in diamond formation, then probably a series of loops, and round it all off with a Lomond inversion. That's quite a favourite with the public.

Sounds real exciting, said the American, setting the exposure on his camera. Why are they called the Red Dragons?

Before the old officer could explain there was a roar from the crowd. The soldiers on the ramparts were checking their equipment. Finishing the jerky sequence they spread their wings again. A hush fell. Traffic on Princes Street stopped. All eyes were on the castle walls.

The soldiers bent their knees and moved their wings slowly up and down. They looked at each other, a few words were exchanged, a strap was adjusted, and they were ready. They sprang into the air and flapped their wings fiercely, hung in the air for an instant, then, seconds later, hit the ground at the bottom of the cliff, one after the other. Through his zoom lens the American saw them break and crumple. In the end they lay strewn, dead or dying, on the grass, their uniforms spoiled with blood, red as red dragons.

The crowd cheered wildly and waved little flags. The old officer clapped, hard and slow, his eyes moist, then turned and walked away. The American looked round. The man he couldn't understand had a look of exultation in his eyes.

Best fucking soldiers in the world, he muttered, gripping the railings. Best fucking soldiers in the world.

* * *

'I got up and crossed the landing and went down stairs. Mind you, if there had been no stairs there I wouldn't even have attempted it.'

Chic Murray
(1919–1985)

Anthony Troon

The Tattoo Reviewed

I don't know what effect the Edinburgh Military Tattoo has upon the enemy, but – by God – it terrifies me. At least its audience does, as we squeeze through the Old Town towards the Castle Esplanade. Not since the castle was blockaded against the Jacobites in 1745 has there been such pushing and shoving as we encounter on Castle Hill these nights. There are approximately 9,000 people involved in this Siege of the Esplanade that occurs before each performance, all of them thinking that it takes only two minutes to walk up Castle Hill – all of them hopelessly misguided.

For most of them, of all nationalities, a visit to the Tattoo might be the only chance they have to observe flesh and blood members of the armed forces going about their business. They sometimes see them on television, encased in tanks, churning across the central German plain on exercises, or they see them dangling on cables from the bellies of helicopters. So, after a visit to the Tattoo, how will the average person's understanding have advanced in the state of the art of war?

Not a great deal, I fear. The only weapons visible at this year's Tattoo are the highly polished rifles, with fixed bayonets, swung around with such abandon by the United States drill team. Certainly, using a rifle in this way is potentially lethal, but the public is entitled to ask whether it is not more efficient to point the thing, and pull the trigger.

Then of course there is the Great Highland Bagpipe, of which well over one hundred examples are paraded in this show, fully distended and in acute song. This has long been recognised as a weapon of war. These days, however, one would have thought that a single piper, linked up to disco-sized amplification, could have fought the battle much more cost-effectively. But who are we to encourage the British Treasury in its budget shrivelling?

Past Tattoos have involved horses, elephants, motor-bikes, tanks, etc., but curiously this year's is conducted entirely on foot. This gives us the chance to observe and marvel over contrasting styles of marching. The piper's and drummer's gait, encumbered by cloth and plumbing, is necessarily a rolling one. The drill team, on the other hand, employs that peculiar, buttock-clenched mincing movement favoured by the American military since passing through the cactus-infested plains of the West made it imperative.

Only one naval officer marches this year, leading out his display team. Naval officers shouldn't be asked to march. The uniform imparts too much urbanity for such militaristic display. A naval officer marching looks like an airline pilot who has been placed under close arrest.

So the Tattoo is a great piece of theatre, beloved of countless spectators – with countless cameras. There is a note in the programme which instructs: 'Photography: the use of flash equipment is expressly forbidden.' Alas, from the very first appearance of the very first pipe major through the castle gate, a rippling electronic barrage begins which persists right through the show. It is the peacetime equivalent of an artillery barrage designed to soften up the infantry. But Malplaquet and Trafalgar were not fought for nothing. In the best traditions of arms, I can report with pride that the allies displayed total steadiness under fire, and fought back to the last alto saxophone.

Neil MacVicar (b. 1953)

Christmas on the Croft with Angus Dreichmore

You know right now I would very gladly be back on the croft up to my neck in all sorts of skeeters just to get away from all this talk about Chrissimus and especially from that clown next door who came to me the other night with his 'Christmas invitation'. By jove if he'd spent the year on the croft like us he'd know what Christmas was all about. Nothing.

I remember the excitement the first time I read all about Christmas and its great celebrations in a book. I asked my grandfather, When is Christmas? Yesterday, he says . . . now get on with your work. Ah, but that wasn't good enough for a young enquiring mind. I kept on.

What's it for? I says. He says, It's to celebrate the birth of our saviour.

Who, the man who brings the seed potatoes, I says?

No, he says. The Almighty Lord of Hosts. Him we go to church to worship for four hours on a Sunday and six if it's the Reverend MacPhail.

So that was it explained, and sure enough the next year we had our very own Christmas. What a set up it was for us youngsters even though we didn't have much in the way of presents. I got a lovely wee rock, but I gave it to my brother Donald because it's better to give than to receive. My grandmother got a lovely scone in a box. My grandfather got most of a sock – the rest of it was used to decorate the tree.

It wasn't a real tree of course. But it was a real piece of fencepost.

Our Christmas meal was fantastic. Herring and potatoes. A real change for us because the rest of the year it was the other way round, and just one of each between us. Then, just when it seemed we could take no more enjoyment my grandmother put her special home-made candle in the middle of the potatoes and we all sang our Christmas song as it crackled and sparked away:

Christmas is an awful curse, Oh damned be this day.
We'd rather be out ploughing stones or drying off
   the hay.
We work the soil and mend the nets and do the best
   we can
But being poor at Christmas means no dumpling in
   the pan.

Now that was a good Christmas. Short and sweet. Over and done with in an hour and then off to work. Not like the claptrap shouting and bawling, bally and hoo you get nowadays when Christmas starts in July and and goes on until June with people sending cards to dogs and snakes and elephants. And these poor brainwashed souls emptying their wallets faster than they can fill their heads with TV nonsense about Christmas presents for the neighbours' cat and women dressing up in wrapping paper.

But the worst of it is, they won't leave normal people alone. The clown next door's 'invitation' was to join his family singing about Good King Wenceslas looking out of a window. Well I drew the line there and then. No clown, I says, no thank you. We never knew anyone called Wenceslas on the croft and looking out windows was something to be ashamed of when there was hard work

Christmas on the Croft with Angus Dreichmore

to be thought about. I certainly won't be dressing up like Santa's sister to go and annoy folk singing about him.

Since when did any of that have anything to do with a poor woman giving birth in a byre? There was no sign of any glittery smittery stupidity then. Just poverty, hunger, misery and desperation. Just the very things which meant the real spirit of Christmas when we were home together on the croft.

* * *

'A Scot is a man who keeps the Sabbath, and anything else he can lay his hands on.'
Chic Murray
(1919–1985)

John Galt (1779–1839)

A Ministerial Debut

The Anno Domini one thousand seven hundred and sixty, was remarkable for three things in the parish of Dalmailing. First and foremost, there was my placing; then the coming of Mrs Malcolm with her five children to settle among us; and next, my marriage upon my own cousin, Miss Betty Lanshaw, by which the account of this year naturally divides itself into three heads or portions.

First, of the placing. It was a great affair; for I was put in by the patron, and the people knew nothing whatsoever of me, and their hearts were stirred into strife on the occasion, and they did all that lay within the compass of their power to keep me out, insomuch, that there was obliged to be a guard of soldiers to protect the presbytery; and it was a thing that made my heart grieve when I heard the drum beating and the fife playing as we were going to the kirk. The people were really mad and vicious, and flung dirt upon us as we passed, and reviled us all, and held out the finger of scorn at me; but I endured it with a resigned spirit, compassionating their wilfulness and blindness. Poor old Mr Kilfuddy of the Braehill got such a clash of glar on the side of his face, that his eye was almost extinguished.

When we got to the kirk door, it was found to be nailed up, so as by no possibility to be opened. The serjeant of the soldiers wanted to break it, but I was afraid that the heritors would grudge and complain of the expense of a new door, and I supplicated him to let it be as it was;

A Ministerial Debut

we were, therefore, obligated to go in by a window, and the crowd followed us, in the most unreverent manner, making the Lord's house like an Inn in a fair day, with their grievous yellyhooing. During the time of the psalm and the sermon, they behaved themselves better, but when the induction came on, their clamour was dreadful; and Thomas Thorl the weaver, a pious zealot in that time, he got up and protested, and said, 'Verily, verily, I say unto you, he that entereth not by the door into the sheepfold, but climbeth up some other way, the same is a thief and a robber.' And I thought I would have a hard and sore time of it with such an outstrapolous people. Mr Given, that was then the minister of Lugton, was a jocose man, and would have his joke even at a solemnity. When the laying of the hands upon me was a-doing, he could not get near enough to put on his, but he stretched out his staff and touched my head, and said, to the great diversion of the rest, 'This will do well enough, timber to timber;' but it was an unfriendly saying of Mr Given, considering the time and the place, and the temper of my people.

After the ceremony, we then got out at the window, and it was a heavy day to me, but we went to the manse, and there we had an excellent dinner, which Mrs Watts of the new inns of Irville prepared at my request, and sent her chaise-driver to serve, for he was likewise her waiter, she having then but one chaise, and that no often called for.

But, although my people received me in this unruly manner, I was resolved to cultivate civility among them; and therefore the very next morning I began a round of visitations; but oh, it was a steep brae that I had to climb, and it needed a stout heart. For I found the doors in some places barred against me; in others, the bairns, when they saw me coming, ran crying to their mothers, 'Here's the feckless Mess-John;' and then when I went in into the houses, their parents would no ask me to sit

John Galt

down, but with a scornful way, said, 'Honest man, what's your pleasure here?'

Nevertheless, I walked about from door to door, like a dejected beggar, till I got the almous deed of a civil reception, and who would have thought it, from no less a person than the same Thomas Thorl that was so bitter against me in the kirk on the foregoing day.

Thomas was standing at the door with his green duffle apron, and his red Kilmarnock nightcap – I mind him as well as if it was but yesterday – and he had seen me going from house to house, and in what manner I was rejected, and his bowels were moved, and he said to me in a kind manner, 'Come in, sir, and ease yoursel; this will never do, the clergy are God's gorbies, and for their Master's sake it behoves us to respect them. There was no ane in the whole parish mair against you than mysel, but this early visitation is a symptom of grace that I couldnae have expectit from a bird out the nest of patronage.' I thanked Thomas, and went in with him, and we had some solid conversation together, and I told him that it was not so much the pastor's duty to feed the flock, as to herd them well; and that although there might be some abler with the head than me, there was na a he within the bounds of Scotland more willing to watch the fold by night and by day.

(from ANNALS OF THE PARISH)

Lewis Grassic Gibbon (1901-1935)

Going Messages For Mistress Munro

Well, Peesie's Knapp and Blawearie were the steadings that lay Stoneheavenway. But if you turned east that winter along the Auchinblae road first on your right was Cuddiestoun, a small bit holding the size of Peesie's Knapp and old as it, a croft from the far-off times. It lay a quarter-mile or so from the main road and its own road was fair clamjamfried with glaur from late in the harvest till the coming of Spring. Some said maybe that accounted for Munro's neck, he could never get the glaur washed out of it. But others said he never tried. He was on a thirteen years' lease there, Munro, a creature from down south, Dundee way, and he was a good six feet in height but awful coarse among the legs, like a lamb with water on the brain, and he had meikle feet that aye seemed in his way. He was maybe forty years or so in age, and bald already, and his skin was red and creased in cheeks and chin and God! you never saw an uglier brute, poor stock.

For there were worse folk than Munro, though maybe they were all in the jail, and though he could blow and bombast till he fair scunnered you. He farmed his bit land in a then and now way, and it was land good enough, the most of it, with the same black streak of loam that went through the Peesie parks, but ill-drained, the old stone drains were still down and devil the move would the factor at Meikle House make to have them replaced, or mend the roof of the byre that leaked like a sieve on the head of Mistress Munro when she milked the kye on a stormy night.

Lewis Grassic Gibbon

But if anybody, chief-like, were to say, *God, that's an awful byre you have, mistress,* she would flare up in a minute *It's one and good enough for the like of us.* And if that body, not knowing better, poor billy, were to agree that the place was well enough for poor folk, she'd up again *Who's poor? Let me tell you we've never needed anybody come to our help, though we don't boast and blow about it all over the countryside, like some I could mention.* So the body would think there was no pleasing of the creature, and she was right well laughed at in all Kinraddie, though not to her face. And that was a thin one and she had black hair and snapping black eyes like a futret, and a voice that fair set your hackles on edge when she girned. But she was the best midwife for miles around, right often in the middle of the night some poor distracted billy would come chapping at her window *Mistress Munro, Mistress Munro, will you get up and come to the wife?* And out she'd get, and into her clothes before you could whistle, and out into the cold of Kinraddie night and go whipping through it like a futret, and soon be snapping her orders round the kitchen of the house she'd been summoned to, telling the woman in childbed she might easily be worse, and being right brisk and sharp and clever.

And the funny thing about the creature was that she believed none spoke ill of her, for if she heard a bit hint of such, dropped sly-like, she'd redden up like a stalk of rhubarb in a dung patch and look as though she might start to cry, and the body would feel real sorry for her till next minute she'd be screeching at Andy or Tony, and fleering them out of the little wits they had, poor devils.

Now, Andy and Tony were two dafties that Mistress Munro had had boarded out on her from an asylum in Dundee, they weren't supposed to be dangerous. Andy was a meikle slummock of a creature, and his mouth was aye open, and he dribbled like a teething foal, and his nose wabbled all over his face and when he tried to speak it was just a fair jumble of foolishness. He was the daftest one, but fell sly, he'd sometimes run away to the hills and stand there with his finger at his nose, making faces at Mistress Munro, and she'd scraich at him and he'd yammer back at her and then over the moor he'd get to the bothy at Upperhill where the ploughmen would give him cigarettes and then torment him till he fair raged; and once tried to kill one with an axe he caught up from a hackstock. And at night he'd creep back to Cuddiestoun, outside he'd make a noise like a dog that had been kicked, and he'd snuffle round the door till the few remaining hairs on the bald pow of Munro would fair rise on end. But Mistress Munro would up and be at the door and in she'd yank Andy by the lug, and some said she'd take down his breeks and skelp him, but maybe that was a lie. She wasn't feared at him and he wasn't feared at her, so they were a gey well-matched pair.

And that was the stir at Cuddiestoun, all except Tony, for the Munros had never a bairn of their own. And Tony, though he wasn't the daftest, he was the queer one, too, right enough. He was small-bulked and had a little red beard and sad eyes, and he walked with his head down and you would feel right sorry for him for sometimes some whimsy would come on the creature right in the middle of the turnpike it might be or half-way down a rig of swedes, and there he would stand staring like a gowk for minutes on end till somebody would shake him back to his senses. He had fine soft hands, for he was no working body; folk said he had once been a scholar and written books and learned and learned till his brain fair softened and right off his head he'd gone and into the poorhouse asylum.

Now Mistress Munro she'd send Tony errands to the wee shop out beyond the Bridge End, and tell him what she wanted, plain and simple-like, and maybe giving him a bit clout in the lug now and then, as you would a bairn or a daftie. And he'd listen to her and make out he minded

Lewis Grassic Gibbon

the messages and off to the shop he'd go, and come back without a single mistake. But one day, after she'd told him the things she wanted, Mistress Munro saw the wee creature writing on a bit of paper with a pencil he'd picked up somewhere. And she took the paper from him and looked at it and turned it this way and that, but feint the thing could she made of it. So she gave him a bit clout in the lug and asked him what the writing was. But he just shook his head, real gowked-like and reached out his hand for the bit of paper, but Mistress Munro would have none of that and when it was time for the Strachan bairns to pass the end of the Cuddiestoun road on their way to school down there she was waiting and gave the paper to the eldest the quean Marget, and told her to show it to the Dominie and ask him what it might mean.

And at night she was waiting for the Strachan bairns to come back and they had an envelope for her from the Dominie; and she opened it and found a note saying the writing was shorthand and that this was what it read when put in the ordinary way of writing: *Two pounds of sugar The People's Journal half an ounce of mustard a tin of rat poison a pound of candles and I don't suppose I can swindle her out of tuppence change for the sake of a smoke, she's certainly the meanest bitch unhung this side of Tweed.* So maybe Tony wasn't so daft, but he got no supper that night; and she never asked to see his notes again.

(from SUNSET SONG)

Alison Kermack   (b. 1965)

Scott's Porrij

ahm noa big fanny
porrij masel
butta bottit fur the bernz
kizzit sayd
thur wizza free gift
inside

turnz oot
the free gift
wizza wee plastic modul
oah nyooklur powur stayshun

now tell me
whittir ma bernz
gonny do
wi that?

*   *   *

> '*I went to the butchers to buy a leg of lamb. 'Is it Scotch?' I asked.*
> '*Why?' the butcher asked. 'Are you going to talk to it or eat it?'*
> '*In that case,' I replied – with as much dignity as I could muster – 'have you got a wild duck?'*
> '*No,' he said, 'but I've got one I could aggravate for you.'*
> Chic Murray
(1919–1985)

David Deans   (b. 1962)

Stone-Age Sheep

Sheep have narrow conelike faces, often grey or black, indicating that their ancestors were perhaps a much swifter moving animal than their modern-day counterpart. The narrow arrowlike structure with an eye each side (hopeless at parallax), allowed for light, nimble gallops over short to medium distances, to catch up with prey (grass), or to evade potential predators, offering the minimum of air resistance. Their flesh, alas, was good and full of proteins, and they quickly accumulated a number of culinary admirers. Mother Nature, however, saw to it that they adapted of themselves, in order to survive, which they obviously have.

The modern sheep foot, or hoof, is but the cloven remnant of an altogether more versatile and zestful appendage that allowed the sheep, given their aerodynamic structures, to travel at speeds that some observers have put at up to sixty miles an hour. And it is the dilemmas raised by these surprising findings that have led some commentators to hypothesise that there were in existence a breed of flying sheep that only became extinct during the middle stone-age. At such great speeds, it is argued, due to its great lumbering upper bulk, plus the skinniness of its paws, the sheep was put under great moral pressure to leave the ground. A branch of these sheep, continues Professor Mackenzie (no relation), located somewhere in modern-day Sutherland, allowed their fleeces to flap at the higher velocities, with the result that they developed

Stone-Age Sheep

special new bone and muscle structures, which could alter (at will) the angle of the fleece, with respect to the angle of the air. Finally they brought their forepaws up as bona fide wings. It is a fearsome notion.

This maverick breed, alas, if we are to believe this theory, and there is no reason why we shouldn't, were not long lived, despite the many obvious advantages in taking to the skies . . .

The fact is, that however ingenious an idea, the sheep was a most clumsy pilot. Under conditions of rain, the fleece was so bogged down with water that the sheep were grounded, running frustrated into the trunks of trees, or, when it was fine, a rare occasion admittedly, their wings would take cramps in the heat of the sun. And even during perfect flying conditions, the sheep's flight was a graceless, half-hearted effort, motivated by sheer (and misplaced) avarice for grass, and the stone-age man, and the stone-age woman, who might have rightly feared and respected the sheep for their courageous take-offs, could only stand aside and mock. And, from rare cave drawings found in the remoter parts of Sutherland, it seems that these unfortunate sheep were endowed not only with the ability to fly but with a similar propensity to that of the common midge, i.e., they were attracted to *Homo sapiens*. God knows why. For whilst the midge thrives off blood, no such motive can be found in the sheep (people did not wear grass). And unless the homo sapiens happened to be in a particularly vulnerable position, say making love to his wife, or there were a particularly large number of approaching sheep (flocks were rare then), in which case the victim would be muffled to death preceded apparently, as in drowning, by pleasant dreamings), it was easy to bat the helpless animals over the snout. The sheep flew at about head height, at approximately five miles an hour, much slower than they ran. No one has yet explained this feat.

David Deans

Around the turn of the neolithic, it appears that 'sheep-batting' had already become a popular sport, widely practised on pitches hewn from peatbogs. Sheep batting can thus be seen as the forerunner to the modern game of cricket, though this is a point of contention. The size of the teams would vary and were often unbalanced. The batters operated in pairs (as in cricket) using a tapering club, and were obliged to wear blindfolds. Otherwise it was too easy. They were therefore obliged to judge their brutal swings purely from the sounds of approaching bleatings. The forerunner to the modern bowler had obviously little part to play in sheep-batting, and it is likely that his role was purely symbolic. At more advanced levels of the game, the fielder was allowed (they had their rules) to 'cat's cradle' the approaching sheep in this deflected direction and that, to further perplex the batters.

The extinction of this tragic species was as much due to the widespread popularity of sheep-battings (or 'happenings' as they were sometimes called), as to the more traditionally held culprits, like the ice age. It is possible that the combined effects of the receding ice-age and the growing popularity of the sport (where the sheep were already more dazed than usual on account of the cold, and less able to survive the game) took a heavy toll among the species, and may have been a decisive factor in their eventual extinction. And it is equally possible that the obscure statute, found in the small print of many a parish to the present day, which prohibits the practice of 'sheepbat' on the sabbath, hitherto regarded as some quirk of obscure origin, derives its origin from this period wherein, through an act of spontaneous clemency, the legendary King Mackenzie (no relation), sought to stem the disappearance of this diverting species.

(from THE PEATMAN)

Anon

'There was a young fellow named Weir . . .'

There was a young fellow named Weir
Who hadn't an atom of fear;
He indulged a desire,
To touch a live wire . . .
Almost any last line will do here.

Alasdair Gray   (b. 1934)

The Trendelenburg Position

Come in, come in, Mrs Chigwell. Sit down. My partner is sorry he cannot attend to you, as arranged, but there will be no complications. His wife was unexpectedly struck down by something this morning and though (thank goodness) she is not exactly at death's door he would find it hard to concentrate on your (thank goodness) smaller problem. His mind might wander, his hand tremble, so you are safer with me. His X-rays indicate two fillings, one of them a wee toaty tiddler of a job, and I am so sure of my skill that I promise you will feel no pain if I work without anaesthetic. But maybe you are nervous and want it, even so? No? Splendid. I am starting the motor – which lowers and tilts the chair – so easily and smoothly that your heart and semi-circular canals have suffered no shock or disturbance. The Trendelenburg Position – that is what we call the position you are in, Mrs Chigwell. This chair gets you into it, and out of it, in a manner which ensures you cannot possibly faint. I wonder who Trendelenburg is.

Or was. Rinse your mouth. Let me – keek – inside. Oho! And if you want to sneeze, gargle, hiccup or blow your nose just raise a finger of your left hand and I will stop what I am doing almost at once but here goes. Chigwell. Chigwell. An English name. Yes there are a lot of your kind in Scotland nowadays, but you'll never hear me complain. Do I bother you, talking away like this? No? Good. You probably realize I do it to stop

The Trendelenburg Position

your imagination wandering, as it would tend to do if I worked in perfect silence. There is, let us face it, something inherently sinister in lying absolutely passive while a stranger in a white coat – no matter how highly qualified – does things you cannot see to this hole in your head – between your jaw and your brain; inside this wee toaty cavity – I am opening – in a bone of your skull. Even the presence of Miss Mackenzie, my assistant here, might not stop your subconscious mind cooking up weird fantasies if we dentists, like barbers, had not a professional tendency to gossip. Which reminds me of a cartoon I saw in a bound volume of old *Punch* magazines : a barber says, 'How would you like your hair cut sir?' to a bored-looking aristocratic type slumped in his chair who says, 'In a silence broken only by the busy snipsnap of the scissors.' Sometimes I hear myself saying ridiculous things, utterly absurd things, just to avoid that deathly silence, but if you prefer silence just raise two fingers of your right hand and silent I will be. But you like the chatter? Good, rinse your mouth again.

No, my worst enemy could never accuse me of being a Scottish Nationalist. I don't approve of Scotland or Ireland – both Irelands – or England, Argentina, Pakistan, Bosnia et cetera. In my opinion nations, like religions and political institutions, have been rendered obsolete by modern technology. As Margaret Thatcher once so wisely said, 'There is no such thing as society,' and what is a nation but a great big example of our non-existent society? Margaret had the right idea – DENATIONAL-IZE! PRIVATIZE! When all our national institutions are privatized the British Isles will no longer be a political entity, and good riddance say I. The USSR has vanished. I hope the USA and the UK follow its example. Last week (a little wider please) a man said to me, 'If you refuse to call yourself a Scot – or a Briton – or a Tory – or a Socialist

Alasdair Gray

– or a Christian what DO you call yourself? What do you believe in?'
'I am a Partick Thistle supporter,' I told him, 'and I believe in Virtual Reality.'
Do you know about Partick Thistle? It is a non-sectarian Glasgow football club. Rangers FC is overwhelmingly managed and supported by Protestant zealots, Celtic FC by Catholics, but the Partick Thistle supporters anthem goes like this:

> We hate Roman Catholics,
> We hate Protestants too,
> We hate Jews and Muslims,
> Partick Thistle we love you . . .

My friend Miss Mackenzie is looking distinctly disapproving. I suspect that Miss Mackenzie dislikes my singing voice. Or maybe she's religious. Are you religious Miss Mackenzie? No answer. She's religious.

Fine. Rinse your mouth. Second filling coming up and I insist on giving you a wee jag, but you won't feel it. Did you feel it? Of course not.

My wife disagrees with me. She's a Scottish Nationalist and a Socialist. Can you imagine a more ridiculous combination? She's a worrier, that woman. She's worried about over-population, industrial pollution, nuclear waste, rising unemployment, homelessness, drug abuse, crime, the sea level, the hole in the ozone layer.

'Only a democratic government responsive to the will of the majority can tackle these problems,' she says. 'How will it do that?' say I. 'By seizing the big companies who are polluting and impoverishing and unemploying us,' says she, 'and using the profits on public work, education and health care.'

The Trendelenburg Position

'You'll never get that,' I tell her, 'because prosperous people don't want it and poor people can't imagine it. Only a few in-betweeners like you believe in such nonsense.' (You have probably guessed she is a school teacher.) 'By the year 2000,' I tell her, 'these problems will have been solved by the right kind of head gear. Even a modern hat of the broad-brimmed sort worn by Australians and Texans and Mexicans will protect you from skin cancer. Hatters should advertise them on television. TO HELL WITH THE OZONE LAYER – WEAR A HAT!'

Hats, Mrs Chigwell, hats. At the start of this century everybody wore them: toppers for upper-class and professional men, bowlers for the middling people, cloth caps for the workers. Bare-headed folk were almost thought as shocking as nudists because their place in the social scale was not immediately obvious. I suspect that hats became unfashionable because we passed through a liberty, equality and fraternity phase – or imagined we were in one. But we're coming out of it again, and by the end of the century everybody will have head gear. Their sanity will depend on it. Am I boring you? Shall I change the subject? Would you like to suggest another topic of conversation? No? Rinse your mouth out all the same.

The hat of the future – in my opinion – will be a broad-brimmed safety helmet with hinged ear-flaps and a mouth-piece which can be folded down to work as a mobile telephone. It will also have a visor like old suits of armour or modern welders have, but when pulled down over your face the inside works as a telly screen. The energy needed to drive these sets could be tapped straight from the action of the viewer's heart – it would use up less energy than walking down a flight of stairs. The difference between one hat and another will be the

Alasdair Gray

number of channels you can afford. The wealthy will have no limit to them, but the homeless and unemployed will benefit too. I am not one of these heartless people who despise the unemployed for watching television all day. Without some entertainment they would turn to drugs, crime and suicide even more than they're doing already, but these video helmets will provide richer entertainment than we get nowadays from these old-fashioned box TVs which to my eyes already look prehistoric – relics of the wood and glass age – BVR – Before Virtual Reality. You've heard about virtual reality? Yes? No? It's a helmet of the sort I've just described. You wear it with a kind of overall suit equipped with electronic pressure pads so that you not only see and hear, but feel you're inside the television world you are watching. Miss Mackenzie is pulling faces at me because she knows what I am going to say and thinks it may shock you since it refers to sex. But I promise that not one bad word will pass my lips. These helmet suits not only give sensations of life and movement in beautiful exciting surroundings. They also, if you desire it, give the visual and sensual experience of an amorous encounter with the partner of your choice. Perhaps Clint Eastwood in your case, Mrs Chigwell, Silvana Mangano in mine, although it shows how old I am. Any professional person who remembers Silvana Mangano in *Bitter Rice* is obviously on the verge of retirement. Or senility. And so, I am afraid, is she. Not that I ever saw her in *Bitter Rice* – a film for Adults Only. I only encountered the first love of my life through her posters and publicity photos. I wonder what Silvana Mangano looks like nowadays?

Excuse me while I wash my hands. We are on the verge of completion. You're still quite comfortable? Good. Here we go again and remember I am talking nonsense, nothing but nonsense.

* * *

The Trendelenburg Position

The hat of tomorrow – an audio-visual helmet with or without the suit – will not only release you into an exciting world of your own choice; it will shut out the dirty, unpleasant future my wife keeps worrying about. It will give marijuana or heavy drug sensations without damaging the health. Of course intelligent people like you and I, Mrs Chigwell, will use it for more than escapist entertainment. We will use it to talk to friends, and educate ourselves. Children of four will be fitted with helmets giving them the experience of a spacious, friendly classroom where beautiful, wise, playful adults teach them everything their parents want them to know. Schools will become things of the past and teachers too since a few hundred well scripted actors will be able to educate the entire planet. And think of the saving in transport! When the lesson stopped they could take the helmet off and bingo – they're home again. Unless the parents switch them onto a babysitter channel.

'All right!' says my wife after hearing me thus far, 'What about homelessness? Your helmets can't shut out foul weather and poisoned air.'

'They can if combined with the right overalls,' I tell her. 'In tropical countries, like India, homeless people live and sleep quite comfortably in the streets. Now, it is a widely known fact that our armed forces have warehouses stacked with suits and respirators designed to help them survive on planet Earth after the last great nuclear war has made everybody homeless. But the last great nuclear war has been indefinitely postponed. Why not add Virtual Reality visors and pressure pads to these suits and give them to our paupers? Tune them into a channel of a warm Samoan beach under the stars with the partner of their choice and they'll happily pass a rainy night in the rubble of a burnt-out housing scheme and please rinse your mouth out. Don't chew anything hard for another couple of hours. The chair – is now restoring you – to a less prone position.

Bye-bye, Mrs Chigwell. The receptionist will give you the bill, and it might be wise to arrange an appointment in – perhaps six months from now. Whatever the future of the human race it is not likely to dispense with dentists.

Robert Crawford (b. 1959)

Alba Einstein

When proof of Einstein's Glaswegian birth
First hit the media everything else was dropped:
Logie Baird, Dundee painters, David Hume – all
Got the big E. Physics documentaries
Became peak-viewing; Scots publishers hurled awa
MacDiarmid like an overbaked potato, and swooped
On the memorabilia: *Einstein Used My Fruitshop,
Einstein in Old Postcards, Einstein's Bearsden Relatives.*
Hot on their heels came the A.E. Fun Park,
Quantum Court, Glen Einstein Highland Malt.
Glasgow was booming. Scotland rose to its feet
At Albert Suppers where The Toast to the General
    Theory
Was given by footballers, panto-dames, or restaurateurs.
In the U.S. an ageing lab-technician recorded
How the Great Man when excited showed a telltale
    glottal stop.
He'd loved fiddlers' rallies. His favourite sport was
    curling.
Thanks to this, Scottish business expanded
Endlessly. His head grew toby-jug-shaped,
Ideal for keyrings. He'd always worn brogues.
Ate bannocks in exile. As a wee boy he'd read
    The Beano.
His name brought new energy: our culture was
    solidly based
On pride in our hero, The Universal Scot.

David Crooks (b. 1955)

Spaced Out

So anyway ah'm just sittin there, havin a wee drink, mindin ma own business, like, and this guy comes up an sits down beside me, an then he says, 'Ye don't mind me sittin here? Naebody's seat, is it?'

'Aye, on ye go,' ah says. No skin off ma porridge, know whit ah mean.

So he starts talkin ti me. Ah don't know whit it is. Must be ma face or somethin. Ah always get the guy in the sheepskin coat that tells ye jokes aboot nuns and Alsatians an that; or the spamheid wi his hair in his pint that starts tellin ye why Russia's no a socialist state.

So ah just sit there, waitin ti see whit this wan wis goany turn oot like. An he says ti me, 'Ye don't mind me talkin ti ye, Jim? Ah'm sayin, ye dinny mind, eh?'

'Naw, sawright,' ah says. Honest, ah wis that bevvied ah didny care.

'Ye see,' he says, 'ah've got somethin ti tell ye. A wee confession, ye know.'

'Fire away,' ah says.

'Well,' he says, 'it's like this. You don't really know who ah am, dae ye?'

So ah looks at him, an ah can see that he isny Adolf Hitler or the Pope, so ah says, 'Naw!'

An he pits doon his pint, and he starts pokin holes in the air, an then he says, 'Ah mean, you just think ah'm an ordinary wee guy, don't ye? Well, ah'm no!'

'Well,' ah says, 'that's fine by me. OK pal?'

42

Spaced Out

'Naw, don't get me wrong,' he says. 'No offence, Jim. Whit ah'm tryin ti say is, it's just that ah'm different.'

'Is that right?' ah says, thinkin he was goany tell me he wis a harry or somethin. Not that ah mind.

So anyway, he says, 'Aye. Actually, ah'm an alien, see?'

Now, ah didny hear him right the first time, so ah got him ti say it again, an even then ah wisny very sure, so ah asked him if he wis foreign or somethin.

'Naw,' he says, 'I come fae Outer Space, ye know.'

Well ah thought he wis jokin. Ah mean, who wouldny? So ah says, 'Ah come fae the Drum. Same thing, intit?'

'Naw,' he says, 'ah'm serious.'

'Aw come on, pal,' ah says, 'pull the other wan, eh?'

'Ye don't believe me, dae ye?' he says. 'Ach well, dinny blame ye.' An then he starts sulkin inti his pint.

So ah takes a good look at him, an sure enough he's just a wee guy wi an old raincoat an baldy hair, an ah can see he likes the bevvy cause he's got a nose like a carrot stump. The pubs are full o' guys like him.

So anyway, ah thought ti masel, May as well have a bit o' a laugh here, eh boys? Ah mean, nothin better ti dae. So ah tellt him ah wis sorry, it was just that ah didny meet an alien every day o' the week, know whit ah mean. An he brightens up, an starts givin me aw this stuff aboot cosmic travel an that.

So ah just sat there deadpan, like, an he's goin on aboot how he's been here for two thousand years, and the place is OK, but he's gettin a bit pissed off, so he's goany shoot the craw, an this is him oot for a last wee drink afore he goes.

Ah mean, it was obvious that the guy's doo-lally, but well, it wis just a laugh, wintit? So ah starts windin him up, an askin him stuff, like whit he's dain here in the first place. An he says he works for this newspaper back in Barnyard Star or somethin like that, which is where

David Crooks

he comes fae, and he got sent here wi bags o' tee-shirts an sunglasses, an folk are supposed ti come up ti him an say, *You are the man from the Barnyard Herald,* and he hands ower the merchandise.

'Is that a fact?' ah says. Ah mean, the guy had some imagination. 'So ye've been hangin roond here for two thousand years, jist waitin?'

'Aye,' he says, 'but naebody ever turned up. Still, a job's a job, intit? Fancy a pint?'

So he goes up ti the bar, an ah'm sittin watchin him, an honest, ye wouldny have thought it ti look at him. An when he gets back, he starts talkin ti me again, but ah canny even mind half o' it. Ah mean, ah'd been in the place since five o'clock. Ah wis miracked! For aw ah knew, it wisny even happenin.

So ah says ti him, 'Whit's it like bein a spaceman, then?'

An he says, 'Ach, it's OK, ah suppose.'

'Whit?' ah says. 'Like Star Wars an that?'

An he starts tellin me how aw they films are mince, an they make spaceships look like Ford Cortinas, nothin but lights an furry dice. 'It's no like that,' he says.

So ah gets him ti tell me aboot his ain spaceship, still havin a good laugh, like, ye know; an he starts comin oot wi aw this crap aboot environmental harmonisation or somethin. Ah mean, ah didny know whit song he wis singin, but he definitely knew aw the words.

'Aye,' he says, 'ah keep it jist along the road. Ye know Glasgow Cross?'

'Oh aye,' ah says. 'Ye mean the polis box?' thinkin that maybe he's been watchin Doctor Who.

'Naw,' he says. 'Ye know that big steeple?'

'Whit? Ye mean, right in the middle?'

'Aye,' he says, 'the Tolbooth. That's it.'

Now that wis definitely worth another pint. So when ah gets back fae tha bar, ah says ti him, 'Right. On ye go. Prove it,' thinkin, well, that's him shattered.

Spaced Out

'Wait a minute,' he says. 'You prove it isny!'

'But it's historical,' ah says. 'In books an that.'

'Ach,' he says, 'anybody can fake history. Dead easy.'

'But it's jist an auld buildin,' ah says. 'Ah even had a piss on it wan night.'

'So what does that prove, except it's waterproof? You ever been in it? Ye ever met anybody that's ever been in it? Well then!'

An he starts going on aboot how naebody can prove nothin, an there's no such thing as facts, an ye've got ti stay septical sic, or else yer mind'll get poisoned wi Science.

'Aw come on,' ah says. 'Science is OK. Science made that pint o'heavy ye were just goany get me.'

'Science,' he says, 'is a big con.'

'Wait a minute,' ah says. 'It aw depends on yer point o' view.'

'That's it exactly,' he says, thumpin the table. 'An that's how it's a con. Aw these guys with their point of view tellin you that they're right. It's like you. You think that just because ah look like an ordinary wee guy that ah am jist an ordinary wee guy, but ah'm no. See whit ah mean? Ye canny go by appearances.'

Ah jist nodded, so he gies me a wee example.

'Right,' he says, 'there's you an Albert Einstein on a train at Glasgow Central, an the train starts movin oot the station at the speed o'light. Ye wi me?'

Ah wis, but ah wished ah wisny.

'So there's two things happens,' he says. 'First, if ye look at that big clock that hings fae the roof, the hands dinny move. Now, Albert says ti himself, "Ya beauty, ve have proved ze theory." But ah'm standing on the platform an ah can see the clock's stopped cause it's needin wound.'

'Is that a fact?' ah says.

'Naw,' he says, 'but the second thing is that cause yer travellin at the speed o'light, the driver thinks the signal at the end o'the platform's green instead o' red, an ye go crashin inti the eight fifteen fae Greenock Central. Wallop!'

So he sits back wi a big grin on his face, an he says, 'An the moral o'this story is: one, Science is garbage; an two, yer better goin by bus.'

'Mine's a pint o'heavy,' ah says.

So when he gets back wi the pints, ah says ti him, 'Two thousand years? 'S a long time, intit?'

'No really,' he says.

'Ye must of seen a few changes,' ah says, wonderin how long he can keep on makin it up.

'Aye,' he says, 'the place just isny the same. No like the old days.' An he starts hittin me wi aw this guff aboot St Mungo, an whit a nice man he wis, an how he helpt him oot wi a few miracles, and how he drew the plans for the Cathedral, an aw the folk he'd met.

'An then there wis Charles Rennie Mackintosh,' he says.

'Oh aye,' ah says, 'Him that invented they digestion pills?' But he jist ignored me.

'Nice guy, so he wis,' he says, 'but no aw that bright. Ah had a go at tellin him aboot four-dimensional architecture, and how it saves queuein for the bog in the mornin, but he couldny get the hang o' it. Tried it in that Art College, an made a right arse o' it.'

'You should be on the telly,' ah says. 'Make a fortune.'

'Worst thing ah ever did,' he says.

'Whit wis that?'

'The telly,' he says.

Well, by this time ah'd had enough. He wisny makin sense, an it wisny jist the bevvy. So ah says ti him, 'Well, it's been nice meetin ye, pal. See ye again sometime,' though ah wisny sure aboot the last bit. But when ah gets ti ma feet, the room starts movin.

'You OK, pal?' he says. 'C'moan ah'll gie ye a hand

Spaced Out

for a taxi.' An he grabs me, an he's askin me whit's the matter.

So ah tellt him. 'It's ma eyes,' ah says. 'Ah'm seein two o' everthin.'

'Well, ye know the reason for that, don't ye,' he says. 'There is two o' everthin. It's only when yer drunk enough that ye see the world as it really is, intit?'

Well, ah couldny argue wi that, could ah? So we gets outside, and the fresh air hits me, and ah'm wonderin whit the hell's goin on.

'Along ti the Cross,' he says. 'That's yer best chance.'

So there we go, doin the Glasgow Foxtrot doon Argyle Street, an he's tellin me how he's goany miss the old place: the bevvy on a Friday night; fish suppers; Hogmanay; Celtic Park on a Saturday.

'You a Tim?' ah says ti him.

'Naw,' he says, 'but ah'm a wee green man!' An he starts laughin. A right comedian, so he wis.

By this time we're jist aboot at the Cross, an ah'm feelin a bit rough, an ah'm busy lookin for a Joe Baxi, but there wisny wan, an then he grabs ma airm, an he says,

'Listen!'

So ah listens, but aw ah can hear is some guyy spewin his ring in a corner.

'D'ye hear it?' he says.

'Whit?'

'The music o' the spheres,' he says, an he jist stands there lookin up inti the sky. So ah'm wonderin whit he's on aboot, so ah looks up, and there's aw these stars, millions o' them; like, just stars, ye know. But then they starts gettin bigger an bigger, till they're like big bright toffee apples or somethin, an ah'm thinkin ti masel, Jeez-oh, must of been a bad pint.

An while aw this is goin on, ah starts hearin it, dead quiet at first, like a kinda singin in ma ears. But then it gets louder, an ah can hear it better, an it wis weird, like

47

David Crooks

somebody takin an eppy on a piana, an ringing bells an playin wi a radio, aw at the wan time.

'Thats's no ma kinda music,' ah says, but he must of went away, cause he didny say nothin. An then there's this noise, like ah'm standin under the Niagara Falls, an the whole world starts meltin or somethin, an the buildins start movin like they're painted on water. Honest, ah wis pure dazzled, so ah wis. An then the next thing ah knew, ah wis lyin flat on ma back, an everythin's stopped movin, an it's quiet again. Ah mean, *really* quiet.

So ah jist kinda lay there for a minute, thinkin ti masel, Well, that's the last time you get bevvied, pal. An then ah hears aw these sirens, an there's aw this commotion, ye know, an some guy's pickin me up, an askin if ah'm OK.

'Ah'm fine,' ah says, an then ah see it's a polis, so ah tellt him ah'd jist fell on the ice, an ah'd be on ma way.

'Haud on,' he says. 'Whit's the score here?' An he points ti this big hole in the road, right in the middle o' the Glasgow Cross.

Well, ye could have slapped me wi a wet kipper.

'Ye'll never believe it,' ah says, an sure enough, he didny.

An so they brought us here, an gave us a cup o' tea, an then you came in an started askin me aw these questions, so ah've tellt ye the story, mister. Jist the way it happened. Honest, it's the truth, so it is. Well, at least ah *think* it is.

Oh, by the way, mister, there isny such a crime as Aidin and Abettin the Theft o' a Historic Buildin. Sure there isny?

Forbes Masson (b. 1964) and
Alan Cumming (b.1965)

Glasgow Song

(*as performed by Victor MacIlvaney and Barry McLeish*)

If you are lonely or suffering from a bereavement,
We know the place you really ought to be.
A town with guts – you see some on the pavement,
High standard of public convenience all for free.
It couldn't be better, it sticks out a mile,
Although it tends to rain a lot the people always smile—
Cos they're guttered!

We're talking Glasgow,
It makes our hearts go funny when we think of it,
Just walk along those streets, see what we mean,
They've been stone-cleaned . . .
Go to fig London!
We're not like you,
We're not capitalists:
You're done in, you took a fall,
When we got the Mahabaratha at the Transport Hall,
Just to cap it all—
Oh oh Glasgow!

It's a cultured city and we don't mean penicillin (*oh
no, oh no*)

Forbes Masson and Alan Cumming

The people have names like Senga, Shug and Lloyd
  (*Senga, Shug and Lloyd*)
Some of them aren't quite the full shilling (*oh no, oh no*)
You'd be the same if you were unemployed.
There's a plethora of parks that have thickets full
  of trees,
Chicken korma comes pre-packed, just take it from the
  freezer for your dinner,
It's a winner—

It's Glasgow,
It makes our hearts go funny when we think of it,
There's no way you can say that Glasgow's past it,
It's been sand blasted . . .
Stuff Auchtermuchty,
We proclaim that Glasgow's got what it takes,
Just take a shufti,
No need to fret,
Or even hedge your bets
You're on an easy win,
If you're Glaswegian,
In Glasgow . . .

(*Spoken*) Glasgow – a city of so many sights, so many smells, so many drinks, so many cigarettes, so many heart attacks, so many happy returns to . . .

Glasgow!
It makes our hearts go funny when we think of it,
Just walk along those streets see what we mean,
They've been stone-cleaned!
Stuff Auchtermuchty,
We proclaim that Glasgow's got what it takes
Just take a shufti,
No need to fret,
Or even hedge your bets

Glasgow Song

You're on an easy win,
If you're Glaswegian,
In Glasgow.

Glasgow *oh oh oh oh oh oh*
Glasgow *oh oh oh oh oh oh*
Gla-la-la-la-la Gla-la-la-la-la Gla-la-la-la-la Glad I live in Glasgow!
Glasgow *oh oh oh oh oh oh*
We belong to Glasgow
Dear old Glasgow toon
Glasgow! Glasgow!

(*During the instrumental reprise – which incidentally is far from being incidental – Victor and Barry wave to their fans, doing their best to hold back the tears. At some point Victor usually faints with the emotion of it all, and as the timpani pound out the last few bars our last image is of Barry begrudgingly dragging Victor into the wings for medical attention, yet still managing a heart-felt smile.*)

Hugh Frater
and Duncan Macrae (1905–1967)

The Wee Cock Sparra

A wee cock sparra sat on a tree,
A wee cock sparra sat on a tree,
A wee cock sparra sat on a tree
Chirpin awa as blithe as could be.

Alang came a boy wi'a bow and an arra,
Alang came a boy wi'a bow and an arra,
Alang came a boy wi'a bow and an arra
And he said: 'I'll get ye, ye wee cock sparra.'

The boy wi' the arra let fly at the sparra,
The boy wi' the arra let fly at the sparra,
The boy wi' the arra let fly at the sparra,
And he hit a man that was hurlin' a barra.

The man wi' the barra cam owre wi' the arra,
The man wi' the barra cam owre wi' the arra,
The man wi' the barra cam owre wi' the arra,
And said: 'Ye take me for a wee cock sparra?'

The man hit the boy, tho he wasne his farra,
The man hit the boy, tho he wasne his farra,
The man hit the boy, tho he wasne his farra
And the boy stood and glowered; he was hurt tae
  the marra.

The Wee Cock Sparra

And a' this time the wee cock sparra,
And a' this time the wee cock sparra,
And a' this time the wee cock sparra
Was chirpin awa on the shank o' the barra.

*   *   *

*'I rang the bell of a small bed-and-breakfast place,
whereupon a lady appeared at an outside window.
"What do you want?" she asked. "I want to stay here," I
replied. "Well, stay there then," she said and banged the
window shut.'*

Chic Murray
(1919–1985)

Arnold Brown   (b. 1936)

The Night Class

The night class at number 15 Abbotsford Place was jam-packed with immigrants. Only the very ambitious ones in the Gorbals were brave enough to attend. They had taken the precaution of studying the new language on the boat coming over. The majority were content to get by with the odd phrase or two, clinging desperately to the Yiddish of the Old Country. That was hardly surprising, considering the impenetrably thick Glasgow accent they encountered everywhere on the streets. Most would wait until their sons and daughters went to school. Parents *can* learn from children . . .

As he was so quick on the uptake, Herschel became the obvious choice to be the family representative at the 'Welcome to Glasgow' series of evening lectures. When you're trying to make it in a new country, you've got to be told the facts, Jimmy.

The lecturer, Mr Andrew McTavish, chalked on the blackboard

WELCOME TO GLASGOW

Tell us everything, Mr McTavish.
He then wrote

GLESGA

'G–L–E–S–G–A. That's another way of spelling the name

The Night Class

of this great city, the Second City of the British Empire. Let me first of all say that you are now living in one of the world's leading industrial centres. One in four of the world's ships and steam locomotives is built here on the Clyde. In the past, we have welcomed other newcomers, like the Highlanders after what was called the 'Clearances'. Luckily we got the Highlanders instead of the sheep. And, of course, we also welcomed into our midst the Irish, who came here after their potato crops failed. And now we are delighted to welcome your people, the Jews, into our community.'

The audience clapped appreciatively.

'But I must be frank. It's not going to be easy for you. There are some customs and traditions which strangers like yourselves will find difficult to understand. I will try to outline the situation as simply as possible.'

He chalked on the board. FOOTBALL (FITBA). 'I will elaborate. There are two great clubs in this city. There's RANGERS. Their ground is Ibrox, team colour light blue, and religion Protestant. And then there's CELTIC. Their ground is Parkhead, their team colour emerald green, and religion Catholic. Oh yes, I nearly forgot. Always remember in Scotland, Protestants are known as "Proddies" and Catholics as "Papes". I'll write that down for you—'

PRODDIES
PAPES

'It is also vital to remember at all times that the Proddies support Rangers and the Papes support Celtic. I'll have to be blunt, lads and lasses. There's a minority of people here in our city, who are what is known as "headcases". But, I repeat, they are a minority.' Mr McTavish chalked up the word 'HEADCASES' on the board. 'In other words, trouble-makers. It obviously follows that it is essential to be able to identify who are Proddies and who are

Papes. To confuse the two groups could place you in a life-threatening situation. Therefore, I suggest for your own safety that if you are asked to comment on the result of any match between Rangers and Celtic, it is absolutely crucial to know firstly which team the person you are talking to supports. And secondly, who won the match, or if it was just a draw. It is very important to know: a mistake could have serious consequences. A slight, intended or otherwise, could leave you in some cases with serious injuries to head, face, chest or legs . . .

'And now, another important point in this connection. If you are passing through the Gorbals and you see at a street corner a group of either Rangers or Celtic supporters assembling, it is etiquette *not* to stare at them.

'The next point I want to bring up here is the "bevvy". I'll write it down for you.'

He chalked it up on the board. B–E–V–V–Y. 'As used in the phrase "Ah'm goin' oot to have a wee bevvy". In other words, a wee dram. A drink. Now I know that your people only imbibe on religious occasions. You are, in effect, teetotallers. But here in Scotland, the working man is traditionally thirsty at the end of a hard day's work, or even if he isn't working, as sometimes does happen. And the Scots, of course, were the ones who invented the most famous drink of them all, whisky. I think I have made it clear how important drink is to the Scottish character. Is it any wonder that many Glaswegians hold teetotallers in such great contempt? So here I must give you another warning about one of our oldest traditions. In Glasgow, we've always enjoyed the ancient ceremony of throwing teetotallers *into* pubs on Saturday nights. I would advise you not to resist the wishes of the Scottish working people. If you allow yourselves to be projected into, say, "The Saracen's Head", and partake of a wee sip of whatever is offered to you, you will allay suspicions that you are spurning hospitality.

The Night Class

'And now Nationalism.'

He chalked the word big and bold on the blackboard.

'The Scots have had many battles with many other nations in the past, but the number one enemy is "The Auld Enemy", England. In Scotland, the English are loathed. No denying it. We hate the buggers . . . Always have and always will. Because of this fact, the worst thing you can do to a Scots person is to attribute the many achievements of his fellow countrymen and women to these English bastards. So as to help you make no embarrassing mistakes, here is a list of Scottish discoveries, past, present and future . . . (I know a very remarkable fortune-teller in the Trongate).'

Mr McTavish walked over to a second larger blackboard and started to list the roll of honour, tears running down his face.

THE MOTOR TYRE – John Boyd Dunlop
THE BICYCLE – Kirkpatrick Macmillan
THE TELEPHONE – Alexander Graham Bell
TELEVISION – John Logie Baird
PENICILLIN – Alexander Fleming
CHLOROFORM – James Young Simpson

Mr McTavish took out a handkerchief from his pocket and dabbed his eyes. 'I'm sorry. Ladies and gentlemen. The mention of so many Scottish geniuses makes me very emotional. Bear with me, please. I'm obliged to tell you of one more custom which you should know about.

'Every 12th July in Glasgow, there's a march by the Protestants through the streets of the city. Pipers. Flute players, drummer boys. Everyone in their regalia, carrying banners. It's to commemorate the victory of the Proddies over the Papes in 1690. William of Orange was the Proddie leader and that's why it's called "The Orange Walk". Now here's the point. The march cannot be interrupted or

Arnold Brown

impeded. So, if you are on the pavement when the march goes by, *stay there and remember, do not attempt to cross the street.* This is Glasgow's Highway Code.

'And now some *good* news for you. After the Orange Walk, sometimes fights break out. Jackets are torn, trousers are ripped, buttons are lost. I know that many of you are tailors, so you might find yourselves inundated with lots of repair jobs. Yes, the Orange Walk could be good for business, so it's not all doom and gloom I'm giving you.

'At the end of each lecture, I'll be introducing you to a well-known Glasgow phrase. That way, you'll be able to participate in the way of life of this great city. I will now write on the blackboard: AWAY AND BILE YOUR HEID. This indicates that you are so angry with someone and have so little respect for them, you are requesting them to go off and boil their head.'

Mr McTavish was coming to the end of his lecture. 'We've covered a lot of ground tonight. I have tried to tell you about the dangers you may encounter. But please do not get the impression that we are a city of violence. The vast majority of our citizens are decent and law-abiding. They want you to share with them all the delights that Glasgow can offer. The fine parks, the magnificent galleries and museums, the elegant tea-rooms, the music-halls, the theatres. Welcome to Glasgow!'

Herschel's hand shot up. 'And also you should say, "Welcome to Glesga!"'

'You catch on quick, Herschel.'

The class enjoyed the exchange and clapped their hands in appreciation. After all, they understood for the first time that they were now citizens of both Glasgow and Glesga.

(from ARE YOU LOOKING AT ME, JIMMY?)

Iain Crichton Smith (b. 1928)

The Story of Major Cartwright, by Murdo

Major Terence Cartwright, wrote Murdo, was an interesting man. He came originally from Hampshire.

When he arrived in the small Highland village of A— his first act was to learn Gaelic. Most of the natives had long ago given up speaking Gaelic but Major Cartwright was determined to keep the old traditions alive. He dressed in the kilt, made crowdie, cut the peats, and had a little dog called Maggie. The dog looked like a dishcloth which you might see on a kitchen table.

At ceilidhs Major Cartwright would introduce the singers and the songs.

'Tha mi toilichte a bhith an seo an nochd,' he would say, speaking with great aplomb. He would insist on speaking Gaelic throughout the ceilidh, though the natives were not used to it.

'We should not let these Sassenachs run our affairs,' he would say, when he spoke English. He voted Scottish Nationalist at all times and would say, 'It is high time we had a government of our own.'

He loved cutting the peats. Everyone else hated doing them: all of them used electricity, gas or coal. But to Major Cartwright cutting peats was the bee's knees. He was never happier than when he was out on the moor among the larks and the midges.

'A fine figure of a man,' the natives would say at first.

Iain Crichton Smith

The Major made oatcakes, which the natives despised. He would hold his little dog in his arms and speak to it in the Gaelic. It looked like the bottom of a mop. *'Tha mi uamhasach toilichte,'* he would say. A few of the natives initially disliked him: then more and more as they saw what he was up to. 'Anyone would think we were living in the eighteenth century, he is bad for our image.'

He advertised lessons in Gaelic but no one went. He wanted to teach the natives the correct use of the dative and the genitive, but they would have none of it. He even began to write poetry in Gaelic, which he published in a national magazine.

'Many is the time,' he would write, 'that I would look over to Harris of the lazybeds. It was there that I was reared.'

The natives thought that they ought to get rid of him. They felt he was riding roughshod over them. His poodle was stolen and Sam Spaid was asked to investigate. Sam Spaid hated the Major at first sight and would only speak to him in English. He found the poodle on a washing line: Anna Maciver, who was eighty years old and almost blind, had hung him there.

'You senile idiot,' said Sam Spaid under his breath. 'You incontinent oaf.' He was wearing a black suit (from Anderson and Sons) and a pair of black shoes (from the Co-op).

'Here is your . . . thing back,' he said to the Major. (You imperialist hound.) The Major made crooning Gaelic noises to the dog, based on a lullaby from Iona.

'What are the marks on my dear Maggie?' said the Major.

'Pegs,' said Sam Spaid curtly.

Sam Spaid went off in a rage to his next case. He had been paid in oatcakes.

The Major began to make oatcakes and crowdie for sale,

The Story of Major Cartwright by Murdo

but no one would buy them. He felt that he was becoming more and more unpopular.

At night, on his own, he read *Dwelly's Dictionary*. He knew the Gaelic for the birds and trees and flowers, shellfish, and so on. Most of the Gaelic speakers from the village had joined the Gaelic Department of the BBC.

The Major had never been so lonely in his life, not even on Salisbury Plain. His wife had stayed in Hampshire and wrote to him in English. He replied in Gaelic. It was with great difficulty that he had managed to take the poodle with him.

'I did not find anywhere more beautiful,' wrote the Major. 'The lochs, the sheilings, the streams.'

He picked up his bagpipes and began to play the 'Lament for the Children.' In the distance he would hear the music from the disco: and someone singing 'Walk Tall' in an American accent.

It was one of his great sorrows that he could not find the Gaelic for 'poodle'.

Night fell over A—. The Major put away his pipes. What had he done wrong? Whenever an Englishman came to the village he would say to him, 'This is not for you. You have done enough harm. Do you know for instance the Gaelic for "rhododendron"?'

The Englishman took the hint. After a while no one stopped in the village, and the bed and breakfast trade failed.

There were murmurings of discontent, rising to open roars of hatred.

'I was born in Uist of the peewit and the rowan,' wrote the Major. The moon shone over *Dwelly's Dictionary*.

One day with his poodle he left. All that was found in his house were some oatcakes, some buttermilk and some crowdie.

He went back to his wife in Hampshire.

Often he would look back on his days in A— with

stunned amazement. He changed his poodle's name from Maggie to Algernon.

'We have seen much together,' he would say to him. 'The time is not yet. The books at the airports are all the same.'

He gave up the bagpipes and gave his kilt to Oxfam. He and his wife opened a restaurant in Hampshire. His oatcakes, buttermilk and herring became famous. The menus were in Gaelic with English translations.

In the evening of his days he would say, 'Fine it was for me that I dwelt once in Harris.' An Indian was chewing his oatcakes with the air of a gourmet and a South Korean was delicately sipping his buttermilk.

'Fine it was for me,' he said, 'that I tasted the salt herring in my youth.'

Doreen Watson

Proposal

Aw goanie?
  Naw acanny
Wi kinyenno?
  Cos acanny
Wi?
  Cos.
Aw goanie?
  Naw
Goan eh?

* * *

'My wife went to the beauty parlour and got a mud pack. For two days she looked nice, then the mud fell off. She's a classy girl, though, at least all her tattoos are spelt right.'

Chic Murray
(1919–1985)

Susan Ferrier (1782–1854)

Scene From a Marriage

> *Though both*
> *Not equal, as their sex not equal seemed –*
> *For contemplation he, and valour formed;*
> *For softness she, and sweet attractive grace.*
> Milton

'What *can* have come over Lady Maclaughlan?' said Miss Grizzy, as she sat at the window in a dejected attitude.

'I think I hear a carriage at last,' cried Miss Jacky, turning up her ears: 'Wisht! let us listen.'

'It's only the wind,' sighed Miss Grizzy.

'It's the cart with the bread,' said Miss Nicky.

'It's Lady Maclaughlan, I assure you,' pronounced Miss Jacky.

The heavy rumble of a ponderous vehicle now proclaimed the approach of the expected visitor; which pleasing anticipation was soon changed into blissful certainty, by the approach of a high-roofed, square-bottomed, pea-green chariot, drawn by two long-tailed white horses, and followed by a lacquey in the Highland garb. Out of this equipage issued a figure, clothed in a light coloured, large flowered chintz raiment, carefully drawn though the pocket holes, either for its own preservation, or the more disinterested purpose of displaying a dark short stuff petticoat, which, with the same liberality, afforded ample scope for the survey of a pair of worsted stockings and black leather shoes, something resembling buckets.

Scene From a Marriage

A faded red cloth jacket, which bore evident marks of having been severed from its native skirts, now acted in the capacity of a spencer. On the head rose a stupendous fabric, in the form of a cap, on the summit of which was place a black beaver hat, tied *à la poissarde*. A small black satin muff in one hand, and a gold-headed walking-stick in the other, completed the dress and decoration of this personage.

The lacquey, meanwhile, advanced to the carriage; and, putting in both his hands, as if to catch something, he pulled forth a small bundle, enveloped in a military cloke, the contents of which would have baffled conjecture, but for the large cocked hat, and little booted leg, which protruded at opposite extremities.

A loud, but slow and well modulated voice, now resounded through the narrow stone passage that conducted to the drawing-room.

'Bring him in – bring him in, Philistine! I always call my man Philistine, because he has Sampson in his hands. Set him down there,' pointing to an easy chair, as the group now entered, headed by Lady Maclaughlan.

'Well, girls!' addressing the venerable spinsters, as they severally exchanged a tender salute: 'so you're all alive, I see; – humph!'

'Dear Lady Maclaughlan, allow me to introduce our beloved niece, Lady Juliana Douglas,' said Miss Grizzy, leading her up, and bridling as she spoke, with ill suppressed exultation.

'So – you're very pretty – yes, you are very pretty!' kissing the forehead, cheeks, and chin of the youthful beauty, between every pause. Then, holding her at arm's length, she surveyed her from head to foot, with elevated brows, and a broad fixed stare.

'Pray sit down, Lady Maclaughlan,' cried her three friends all at once, each tendering a chair.

'Sit down!' repeated she; 'why, what should I sit down

for? I choose to stand – I don't like to sit – I never sit at home – Do I, Sir Sampson?' turning to the little warrior, who, having been seized with a violent fit of coughing on his entrance, had now sunk back, seemingly quite exhausted, while the *Philistine* was endeavouring to disencumber him of his military accoutrements.

'How very distressing Sir Sampson's cough is!' said the sympathising Miss Grizzy.

'Distressing, child! No – it's not the least distressing. How can a thing be distressing that does no harm? He's much the better of it – it's the only exercise he gets.'

'Oh! well, indeed, if that's the case, it would be a thousand pities to stop it,' replied the accommodating spinster.

'No, it wouldn't be the least pity to stop it!' returned Lady Maclaughlan, in her loud authoritative tone; 'because, though it's not distressing, it's very disagreeable. But it cannot be stopped – you might as well talk of stopping the wind – it is a cradle cough.'

'My dear Lady Maclaughlan!' screamed Sir Sampson, in a shrill pipe, as he made an effort to raise himself, and rescue his cough from this aspersion; 'how can you persist in saying so, when I have told you so often it proceeds entirely from a cold caught a few years ago, when I attended his Majesty at—' Here a violent relapse carried the conclusion of the sentence along with it.

'Let him alone – don't meddle with him,' called his lady to the assiduous nymphs who were bustling around him, – 'Leave him to Philistine; he's in very good hands when he is in Philistine's.' Then resting her chin upon the head of her stick, she resumed her scrutiny of Lady Juliana.

'You really are a pretty creature! You've got a very handsome nose, and your mouth's very well, but I don't like your eyes, they're too large and too light; they're saucer eyes, and I don't like saucer eyes. Why ha'nt you black eyes? you're not a bit like your father – I knew him very well. Your mother was an heiress, your father married her for her money, and she married him to be a Countess, and so that's the history of their marriage – humph.'

This well-bred harangue was delivered in an unvarying tone, and with unmoved muscles; for though the lady seldom failed of calling forth some conspicuous emotion, either of shame, mirth, or anger, on the countenances of her hearers, she had never been known to betray any correspondent feelings on her own; yet her features were finely formed, marked, and expressive; and, in spite of her ridiculous dress and eccentric manners, an air of dignity was diffused over her whole person, that screened her from the ridicule to which she must otherwise have been exposed. Amazement at the uncouth garb and singular address of Lady Maclaughlan, was seldom unmixed with terror at the stern imperious manner that accompanied all her actions. Such were the feelings of Lady Juliana, as she remained subjected to her rude gaze, and impertinent remarks.

'My Lady!' squeaked Sir Sampson from forth his easy chair.

'My love?' interrogated his lady as she leant upon her stick.

'I want to be introduced to my Lady Juliana Douglas; so give me your hand,' attempting, at the same time, to emerge from the huge leathern receptacle into which he had been plunged by the care of the kind sisters.

'O pray sit still, dear Sir Sampson,' cried they as usual all at once; 'our sweet niece will come to you, don't take the trouble to rise; pray don't,' each putting a hand on this man of might, as he was half risen, and pushing him down.

'Aye, come here, my dear,' said Lady Maclaughlan; 'you're abler to walk to Sir Sampson than he to you,' pulling Lady Juliana in front of the easy chair; 'there – that's her; you see she is very pretty.'

'Zounds, what is the meaning of all this!' screamed the

enraged baronet: 'My Lady Juliana Douglas, I am shocked beyond expression at this freedom of my Lady's. I beg your Ladyship ten thousand pardons; pray be seated. I'm shocked; I am ready to faint at the impropriety of this introduction, so contrary to all rules of etiquette. How *could* you behave in such a manner, my Lady Maclaughlan?'

'Why, you know, my dear, your legs may be very good legs, but they can't walk,' replied she, with her usual *sang froid*.

'My Lady Maclaughlan, you perfectly confound me,' stuttering with rage. 'My Lady Juliana Douglas, see here,' stretching out a meagre shank, to which not even the military boot and large spur could give a respectable appearance: 'You see that leg strong and straight,' stroking it down; 'now, behold the fate of war!' dragging forward the other, which was shrunk and shrivelled to almost one half its original dimensions. 'These legs were once the same; but I repine not – I sacrificed it in a noble cause: to that leg my sovereign owes his life!'

'Well, I declare, – I had no idea; – I thought always it had been rheumatism,' burst from the lips of the astonished spinsters, as they crowded round the illustrious limb, and regarded it with looks of veneration.

'Humph!' emphatically uttered his lady.

'The story's a simple one, ladies, and soon told: I happened to be attending his Majesty at a review; I was then aid-de-camp to Lord—. His horse took fright, I – I – I,' – here, in spite of all the efforts that could be made to suppress it, the *royal cough* burst forth with a violence that threatened to silence its brave owner for ever.

'It's very strange you will talk, my love,' said his sympathising lady, as she supported him; 'talking never did, nor never will agree with you; it's very strange what pleasure people take in talking – humph!'

'Is there any thing dear Sir Sampson could take?' asked Miss Grizzy.

Scene From a Marriage

'*Could* take? I don't know what you mean by *could* take. He couldn't take the moon, if you mean that; but he must take what I give him; so call Philistine, he knows where my cough tincture is.'

'Oh, we have plenty of it in this press,' said Miss Grizzy, flying to a cupboard; and, drawing forth a bottle, she poured out a bumper, and presented it to Sir Sampson.

'I'm poisoned!' gasped he, feebly; 'that's not my Lady's cough-tincture.'

'Not cough-tincture!' repeated the horror-struck doctress, as for the first time she examined the label; 'O! I declare, neither it is – it's my own stomach lotion. Bless me, what will be done!' and she wrung her hands in despair. 'Oh Murdoch,' flying to the *Philistine*, as he entered with the real cough-tincture, 'I've given Sir Sampson a dose of my own stomach lotion by mistake, and I am terrified for the consequences!'

'Oo, but hur need na be feared, hur will no be a hair the war o't; for hurs wad na tak' the feesick that the leddie ordered hur yestreen.'

'Well, I declare things are wisely ordered,' observed Miss Grizzy; 'in that case, it may do dear Sir Sampson a great deal of good.'

Just as this pleasing idea was suggested, Douglas and his father entered, and the ceremony of presenting her nephew to her friend, was performed by Miss Grizzy in her most conciliating manner.

'Dear Lady Maclaughlan, this is our nephew Henry, who, I know, has the highest veneration for Sir Sampson and you. Henry, I assure you, Lady Maclaughlan takes the greatest interest in every thing that concerns Lady Juliana and you.'

'Humph!' rejoined her Ladyship, as she surveyed him from head to foot: 'So your wife fell in love with you, it seems; well, the more fool she, I never knew any good come of love marriages.'

Susan Ferrier

Douglas coloured, while he affected to laugh at this extraordinary address, and withdrawing himself from her scrutiny, resumed his station by the side of his Juliana.

'Now, girls, I must go to my toilette; which of you am I to have for my handmaid?'

'O! we'll all go,' eagerly exclaimed the three nymphs; 'our dear niece will excuse us for a little; young people are never at a loss to amuse one another.'

'Venus and the Graces, by Jove!' exclaimed Sir Sampson, bowing with an air of gallantry; 'and now I must go and adonise a little myself.'

The company then separated to perform the important offices of the toilette.

(from MARRIAGE)

Will Fyffe (1885–1947)

The Scot's Lament

I'm Scotch and I'm married, two things I can't help,
   I'm married – but I have no wife—
For she bolted and left me – but that's nothing new,
   It happens sa often in life.
So I journeyed ta London, for that's where she'd gone
   With her lover to hide her disgrace.
And though London's a big town I swore I'd not rest
   Till I'd searched every street in the place.
And I tramped – how I tramped – weary mile upon mile
   Till exhausted and ready ta drop.
I would not give in, so I climbed on a bus,
   And took a front seat on the top.
We came to a halt in a brightly lit square
   To my joy, there ma lassie I spied,
Looking weary and worn, but thank heaven – ALONE—
   From my heart – 'Maggie – Maggie' I cried.
She gasped with delight as I rose from ma seat,
   But a harrowing thought made me wince,
I couldna get off – for I'd just paid ma fare,
   AND I'VE NEVER CAUGHT SIGHT OF HER SINCE.

Neil Munro (1863–1930)

Linoleum

Mr James Swan has lived for fifteen years in Ibrox. For the first six months he thought it horrible, and ever since he has vexed himself to think how foolish he was not to have gone there sooner. That is life. Men are like pot plants. You shift a geranium into a new pot, and for weeks it wilts disconsolate, till some fine sunny day it seems to realise that other geraniums seem happy enough in the same sort of pots, and that it isn't the pot that matters really. Whereupon the geranium (which is actually a pelargonium) strikes fresh roots into the soil, spreads out a broader leaf, throws out a couple of blossoms, and delights in making the best of it. It takes the first prize at the local flower show; content is the best fertiliser. Jimmy Swan, after fifteen years at Ibrox, thinks Ibrox is the centre of the solar system. Take him to Langside or Partickhill, and he feels chilly; at Dennistoun he feels himself a foreigner, and looks at passing tramcars for the Southside as an exile from Scotland, haunting the quays of Melbourne, looks at ships from the Clyde with the names of Denny or Fairfield on their brasses. Jimmy said to me the other day, 'I canna think how people can live ony where else than Ibrox. It's the best place in the world.' 'How?' I asked. 'Well,' said he, 'it's-it's-it's-it's Ibrox!' A little inconclusive, but I quite understood. Nine-tenths of us have our Ibrox; the people to be sympathised with are those who haven't.

But Jimmy got an awful start the other day! He came home from the North journey on a Saturday very tired,

Linoleum

and exceedingly glad to see the familiar streets of Ibrox again. Nothing had changed; the same ham was in the grocery window, apparently only a slice the less, and he had exactly the high tea he expected, but his wife was different. She plainly nursed some secret discontent. Quite nice, and interested in his journey, and all that, but still . . .

It turned out to be the linoleum. The lobby linoleum. She put it to Jimmy if a lobby linoleum seven years old could honestly be regarded as quite decent.

'Tuts! there's naething wrang wi' the linoleum,' said her husband. 'As nice a linoleum as anybody need ask for; I never tripped on't yet.'

'The pattern's worn off half of it,' said his wife; 'Mrs Grant was in today, and I was black affronted. In her new house in Sibbald Terrace they have Persia rugs.'

'Kirkcaldy's good enough for us,' said Jimmy; 'just you wait for a year or twa and ye'll see the fine new linoleum I'll get ye.'

It was then that the shock came. Mrs Swan, having brooded for a while on the remoteness of a new linoleum, intimated with a calm that was almost inhuman that she had been looking at some of the houses to let in Sibbald Terrace. Their present house had become no longer possible. It had all the vices conceivable in any house built of human hands, and several others peculiar to itself, and evidently of their nature demoniac. It was cold, it was draughty, it was damp, it was dismal. Its chimneys did not draw properly; its doors were in the wrong places; its kitchen range was a heartbreak; its presses were inadequate – she took ten minutes to expose all its inherent defects as a dwelling, and left her astonished listener in the feeling that he had been living for fifteen years in an orange-box without knowing it.

'We'll have to flit!' she said at last, determinedly. 'Sibbald

Terrace is no' in Ibrox!' said her husband, astonished at her apparent overlook of this vital consideration.

'All the better o' that!' said the amazing woman. 'I'm sick o' Ibrox! You can say what you like, James Swan; I'll no' stay another year in this hoose.'

'Ye're fair fagged oot, Bella,' said her husband, compassionately. 'I doubt ye have been washin', efter all I told ye. Ye should stay in your bed the morn, and never mind the kirk. Sick o' Ibrox? Ye shouldna say things like that even in fun!'

It was at this stage, or a few days after it, I met Mr Swan. He was chuckling broadly to himself. 'Did you ever flit?' he asked me.

'Once,' I said.

'That's enough for a lifetime,' said he. 'Men would never flit any mair than they would change their sox if it wasna for their wives. The advantage o' an auld hoose is that ye aye ken where your pipe is. My wife took a great fancy to flit the other day, and I said it was a' right; that I would look out for a new house. At the end o' three days I said I had a fair clinker – vestibule wi' cathedral glass in the doors, oriel windows in the parlour, fifteen by eight lobby, venetian blinds, bathroom h. and c., wash-hand basin electric light, tiled close, and only five stairs up.

'She says, "Do ye think I'm daft? Five stairs! Is it in the Municipal Buildin's?"

'"No," says I; "it's in Dalwhinnie Street."

'"Where in a' the earth is Dalwhinnie Street?" says she.

'"It's a new street," I said, "near Ruchill. Ye take the car from about the foot o' Mitchell street, come off at an apothecary's shop, and take the first turn to the right and ask a message-boy."

'"I'll not go to any such street, James Swan!" she says; I would rather take a place!' and the dear lass was a' trimblin' wi' agitation."

Linoleum

'No wonder, Mr Swan,' I said. 'It sounded a very out-of-the-way locality. Where is Dalwhinnie Street?'

'There's no such street,' said Mr Swan: 'at least if there is, I never heard o't. But ye see I wanted to put her aff the notion o' flittin'. And there was Bella, almost greetin'! I let on I was fair set on Dalwhinnie Street because it was so handy for the Northern Merchants' Social Club. But Dalwhinnie Street, right or wrong, she would not hear tell o', and I said I would take another look round.'

Mr Swan cocked his head a little and looked slyly at me. 'Ye're a married man, yoursel',' said he. 'Ye know what wives are. They're no' such intellectual giants as we are, thank God! or else they would find us out; but once they've set their minds on a thing, Napoleon himself couldna shift them. Some days after that I cam' hame from Renfrewshire wi' a great scheme for takin' a house in the country. I said I had seen the very house for us – half-way between Houston and Bridge-of-Weir.'

'"Whereabouts is Houston?" says the mistress in frigid tones, as they say in the novels.

'"It's half-way between the Caledonian and G. and S.W. lines," says I, "and if ye're in a hurry ye take a 'bus if it's there."

'"What sort o' house is it?" she asked, turnin' the heel o' a stockin' as fast as lightning.

'"Tip-top!" I says. "Nine rooms and a kitchen; fine flagged floor in the kitchen; spring water frae the pump in the garden; two-stall stable. Any amount o' room for hens; ye can keep hunders o' hens. The grocer's van passes the door every Thursday."

'She began to greet. "That's right!" she says. "Put me awa' in the wilds among hens, so that I'll die, and ye'll can marry a young yin. But mind you this, James Swan; I'll no' shift a step oot o' Ibrox!"

'"Tuts, Bella!" I says, "ye canna stay ony langer in this house; it's a' wrang thegither."

'"There's naething wrang wi' the hoose," says she, "if I had jist some fresh linoleum."

'"Well, well," says I; "ye'll get the linoleum" – and I was much relieved. "I'll buy't to-morrow." And I did. It cost me 4s. 6d. a yard.'

'Your wife is a very clever lady, Mr Swan,' I said; 'she probably never thought of flitting, but badly wanted that linoleum.'

'Of course!' said Jimmy Swan. 'I kent that a' alang! But ye've got to compromise!'

Harry Ritchie   (b. 1958)

Brief Encounter

It *was* him. He was window-shopping, oddly enough, outside the Boutique Esmerelda, intrigued by its selection of hats and beachwear. He himself was sporting, somewhat uncharacteristically, a migrainous shirt and purple patterned shorts.

I couldn't pass up the chance to talk to him. I *had* to do this.

'Mr Connery,' I said as I approached. 'Can I just say what a very great pleasure it is to meet you?'

There was, I swear, more than a hint of a demure smile below his quizzical frown. (He really was astonishingly handsome.) Encouraged, I persevered.

'Perhaps I could offer you a drink? Actually, I'm writing something about Marbella and I'd be hugely grateful if I could ask you a few questions.'

He still said nothing in reply, but there was still that hint of a smile.

'But if you don't want to be pestered, I'd quite understand. Please, though, let me buy you a drink. You've always been, well, one hesitates to say role model, but certainly a hero of mine.'

For a moment, Sean looked utterly baffled. What would he say? 'Come over to my house for a drink' would be ideal. But a 'shplendid to meet you' would be more than enough. What Sean actually did was shrug and point towards a sign for the Oficina de Turismo.

'*Paracaracarosamente*,' he said, before smiling helpfully and walking away.

Harry Ritchie

It was an understandable mistake, honestly. For a kick-off, it there had been a Sean Connery Lookalike Contest, the great man himself would have been pipped for first place by that guy. And anyway, I continued to reason, as I put my head in my hands and tried not to curl up into the embryo position, Marbella is supposed to be the haunt of the rich and famous, and, famously, of Sean Connery. Cilla Black had been spotted the week before at a restaurant just up the road. Bruce Forsyth, alas, has a place just outside town.

And Jimmy Tarbuck. And Shirley Bassey, who was said to have been sighted recently near one of the prom's amusement arcades. I'd met people who'd known people who'd definitely seen Sean Connery walking around the town, just like a person.

But I should have guessed he wasn't really him. It was too much like good luck, on my second day, bumping into the one man I would have killed to bump into. The shirt was a bit of a giveaway, I suppose. And, on reflection, it had to be admitted that Sean Connery has never been the sort to wear purple patterned shorts.

(from HERE WE GO: A SUMMER ON THE COSTA DEL SOL)

* * *

'I am very glad to have seen the Caledonian Canal, but don't want to see it again.'

Matthew Arnold
(1822–1888)

Kate Atkinson (b. 19??)

1964: Holiday!

We're off! Not to see the wizard, but on holiday. 'We're off!' I say enthusiastically to Patricia.
'Shut up, Ruby!'
Shutupruby, shutupruby. Honestly, you'd think that was my name in the World According to Patricia. She's busy drawing obscene anatomical diagrams on the misted-up insides of the car windows. It's cold and damp both inside and outside the car – a weather situation that doesn't seem a good omen for our impending holiday. The self-catering years (Bridlington, Whitby) are over and the exotic destinations lie ahead of us (Sitges, North Wales) beginning with, possibly the most foreign location of all – Scotland! . . .

The occupants of the farm, our hosts for the next two weeks, are called von Leibnitz, which doesn't seem like a very Scottish name to me. Wouldn't we have done better to have chosen a Farm from the Farmhouse Brochure that was run by a McAllister, a Macbeth, a McCormack, a McDade, a McEwan, a McFadden – even a McLeibnitz – in fact anyone whose name began with a 'mac' rather than a 'von'? Mr von Leibnitz ('Heinrich'), we discover later on, was a German POW who was sent to work on the farm and stayed on, marrying the farmer's widow – Mrs von Leibnitz – or Aileen McDonald as she was before her husband died in North Africa and was substituted by the enemy. This, together with the fact that Mrs von Leibnitz came originally from Aberdeen, makes them a pair of total outsiders in Och-na-cock-a-leekie, which perhaps accounts for their stern character. 'So it was old McDonald's farm then?' George jokes, on hearing this story, but is met with stony countenances from the von Leibnitzes. They have no sense of humour whatsoever – even Bunty has a sense of humour compared with our hosts. They have united Prussian gloom and Presbyterian dourness in an awesome combination. Spare and tall, straight-backed and solemn, they clearly regard holidaymakers as frivolous, weak creatures. Perhaps they're right.

There is a lot of fuss about bedrooms, reminiscent of the dilemma over taxonomies in the Spirit World. How will we be permutated? Boys with boys, girls with girls? Roper with Roper, Lennox with Lennox? And what of the adults – husband with wife? Or not? Mrs Roper dispatches us with efficiency, while Bunty exchanges lingering looks with Mr Roper. 'Shall I carry that for you, Bunty?' he asks soulfully, and, reaching for a suitcase, their fingers meet for an achingly long time, until, in fact, they are bodily separated by Patricia, barging up the stairs between them and grabbing the suitcase on her way.

Mrs Roper puts all the girls together in an attic bedroom that reeks of must, and Patricia makes a dive for the single bed, leaving me to share the double with Christine, who spends half of every night telling me to move up, even though I'm already sleeping on the edge, and the other half grinding her teeth and muttering in her sleep.

For our first breakfast, seated at a long, dark-oak table in a gloomy, cold dining-room, we are served plates of lukewarm, salty porridge (to Patricia's dismay) with neither milk nor sugar, and afterwards a strip of bacon each and a little pile of cold baked beans. This is prison food, not holiday food.

'*Cold* baked beans?' Bunty puzzles.

'Maybe that's how the Scots eat them,' Mr Roper

1964: Holiday!

suggests, 'or the Germans,' he adds as an afterthought. I think it was at this moment that Patricia lurched from the table, informing everyone that she was going to be sick and indeed was as good as her word, throwing up before reaching, the door ('Heinrich, fetch a clout – the lassie's boaked!'). And she hasn't even eaten any breakfast yet! We have been on holiday less than twenty-four hours and three people have vomited already. How many more times will this happen? (Many.)

And from there it's downhill all the way. There isn't very much to do on the farm; you can look at the five cows, whose milk goes straight to the dairy, not to our porridge, and you can annoy the four chickens, whose eggs go straight into a tarred barrel of water-glass, and you can survey a couple of damp, rain-flattened fields of barley, but after that there isn't much left, apart from the sheep, scattered like little limestone outcrops over rolling, humpy hills of brown-green grass and bracken.

In the distance, over those hills and far away, at the outer barriers of the von Leibnitz property, is where the real Scotland seems to be (I have read *Rob Roy* and *Waverley* and *The Heart of Midlothian* in preparation for this trip), a swathe of purple and lilac rising up to the horizon and melting into the sky, cloaked on one side by a forest of bristling, bottle-green trees. 'Aye,' says Mr von Leibnitz, in a more forthcoming mood than usual, 'dat's partov di ancient Caledonian Vorest,' and my heart leaps because this sounds more like Scott's Scotland. ('It's funny, isn't it, that he was called Scott, when he *was* a Scot,' I venture conversationally to Mrs von Leibnitz when I'm abandoned to her care on Black Tuesday – of which more later, unfortunately – but she responds, 'You're a gey peculiar wee lassie, are you no?' because she doesn't read anything except *The People's Friend*.)

We are rather surprised to find that we aren't near the

sea and there's quite a lot of discussion about whose fault this might be, Mr Roper's orienteering skills once more being brought into disrepute by George (and defended by his mistress). Several day trips are planned to visit not only the sea but other places of 'historic and architectural interest' – Mrs Roper has brought a guide-book with her – and our first expedition is to Fort William via the famous Glencoe. 'Why is it famous?' I ask Mrs Roper, who is peering at the guide-book in one hand while wafting one of the baby-David's dirty night-nappies in the other. 'A massacre,' she says vaguely.

'A massacre,' I tell Patricia.

'Oh good,' she says with relish.

'No, no,' I say hastily, 'an historical one,' but you can see from the look in her eye that Patricia isn't thinking about Campbells and McDonalds, but Ropers and Lennoxes. Or perhaps just Lennoxes.

A black cloud, both metaphorical and real, settles above our heads as we enter Glencoe. ('Aye,' Mrs von Leibnitz confirms later, 'it's an uncanny dreich place that Glencoe.') The hills rise, grim and threatening, on either side of us but we arrive safely, *sans* massacre, and sample the delights of Fort William on a rainy day. We take immediate cover in another Kitchen, a 'Highland' one this time, which is full of people and pushchairs, sopping macs and dripping umbrellas, and a chrome *Gaggia*, hissing aggressively. The grown-ups, as they comically refer to themselves, have coffee in glass cups and saucers and Bunty smiles across the red tinfoil ashtray at Mr Roper and says, 'Sugar, Clive?' holding out the stainless-steel pot as if it contained Aphrodite's golden apples and not brown-sugar crystals. 'Thank you, Bunty,' he says, locking his smile onto hers while the rest of us watch his spoon as if we're hypnotized, as he stirs it round and round and round and round and round and round until Mrs Roper says suddenly, 'You don't take sugar, Clive!' and we all wake up.

1964: Holiday!

Patricia sips feebly at a glass of water, I have a cup of tea, Christine has milk, Kenneth has a Fanta and the baby-David is allowed a banana milk-shake which Mrs Roper pours into his baby-cup. The banana milk-shake is a sickly yellow colour that seems to owe very little to a bunch of Fyffes and it comes as no surprise to me when he dribbles most of it back up again after a few minutes. Patricia retires with precipitate haste behind a door marked 'Lassies' but everyone else, I'm glad to say, manages to hold their liquids down.

We discover that we've left the guide-book in Ochna-cock-a-leekie and wander the streets disconsolately, looking for something of architectural or historical interest, settling eventually on the Wee Highland Gift Shop where we buy many totally useless objects adorned with thistles and heather, although personally, I am delighted with my *Illustrated Pocket Guide to Scottish Tartans*, even if half the tartans are reproduced in hazy black-and-white. Foolishly, we buy sugar in large quantities – Whisky Fudge, Soor Plums (a Scottish delicacy, the woman in the shop tells us), Edinburgh Rock and long ropes of shiny liquorice. A sudden, painful August hailstorm prompts a group decision to abandon the Fort and we scamper back to the car park, and take the high road back to the Farmhouse.

On the journey back, we set about consuming our newly-bought confectionary in lieu of lunch and it isn't long before the Ropers' car is drawing up at the side of the road (*He's stopping!*) for the baby-David to splatter the remains of his banana-yellow vomit all over the grass verge and, two minutes after we're off! for the second time, it's our turn because the lassie's boaking again. Even the normally stalwart Mrs Roper has to 'take some fresh air' under the lowering skies of Glencoe. 'Poor Harriet,' George says, causing Bunty to look at him in speechless astonishment because he has never said 'Poor Bunty'

Kate Atkinson

in his life, but she never gets round to articulating this astonishment because Patricia moans gently and we have to *Stop!* again.

I commiserate with her, 'Nobody knows the trouble you've seen, Patricia.'

'Shutupruby.'

(from BEHIND THE SCENES AT THE MUSEUM)

*   *   *

'It requires a surgical operation to get a joke well into a Scotch understanding – their only idea of wit . . . is laughing immoderately at stated intervals.'

Sydney Smith
(1771–1845)

Ludovic Kennedy   (b. 1919)

A Hole in One

In humour the Scots and English have a quite different approach. A saying of the English savant Sydney Smith that it would take a surgical operation to drive a joke into a Scotsman's head has been much quoted and, in Scotland, much resented. What he meant, and should have said, was *an English joke*. English jokes, like the English, tend to be more sophisticated.

Most humour is based on human failings and Scots humour more than most. For instance, a golfer playing the first hole at St Andrews drove six balls one after the other into the notorious Swilcan burn. As he and his caddy walked forward to retrieve them, the golfer said, "I'm going to drown myself in that burn." The caddy said (another example of Scottish classlessness), "You couldny." "Why not?" "Ye couldny keep your heid doon lang enough."

(from IN BED WITH AN ELEPHANT)

Muriel Gray   (b. 1959)

Cutting a Dash

If you intend to escape from the teeming folly of city life and hightail it to the freedom of the hills, does it really matter what you wear? Of course it matters. You might think you're safe nipping out for a hill-walk in a Parka with nylon fur round the hood, and a pair of trawlerman's oilskin trousers you bought at a life-boat fund-raising stall, but that's the day you'll bump into Sean Connery and Christopher Lambert with a film crew making *Highlander 3*. If you're a male reader, you can reverse this law of probability, and be sure that you will meet Madonna doing a nude shoot for the Pirelli calendar on Ben Vorlich.

Unlikely as it seems, mountain vanity is rife. It's not enough any more to have comfortable boots and something waterproof to slip over a jumper. Your attire must tell other walkers and climbers how serious you are, indicate the status you enjoy in the world of mountaineering, and not make locals in the mountain's nearest bar fall dangerously silent when you pop in for a pint on the way back home.

For instance, let's take grey anoraks. The lust for grey anoraks in a profound sickness. The garments are usually shapeless, not very waterproof, and can be worn only with an olive-green acrylic hat, long, brown woollen slacks, and a pair of stout shoes from British Home Stores. Displayed in this manner, the grey anorak will serve its purchaser well, by having him ordered off the hill by

Cutting a Dash

Mountain Rescue before his car boot is slammed shut. If the owner is unfortunate enough to have a fall, the grey anorak will help him resemble a large rock when the RAF hover above, thus rendering him practically invisible. One can only assume that the purchasers of these lichen-grey accoutrements are members of EXIT, and that anyone attempting to rescue them would receive a bloody nose for their trouble. What other explanation could there possibly be for going into a shop, flicking through rails of attractive fuchsia, cobalt and aquamarine outer-garments, and saying to the assistant, 'Have you got any grey ones?'

Perhaps the shopkeeper should have a panic button under the counter to press during such a confrontation, and while humouring the shopper by pretending to go and look for some grey ones, stout men could rush in and restrain the customer before he can make it to his Access card. It's not as if grey anoraks are cheap. Since they are hard to find, except in odd little shops that specialise in big underpants for old people and sheepskin slippers, they cost a pretty penny. A certain firm famous for their 'bags' trouser suits, used to do an extensive line of grey anoraks, but they obviously had a visit from the style police and were made to put bits of navy blue and red in them or face a lengthy jail sentence. Not exactly Jean Paul Gaultier, but it's a start.

Of course it's possible to go too far the other way, a natural but perilous reaction to grey anorak anxiety, in fact a sort of anoraksia nervosa. Such hill-walkers are uncomfortable unless they look like the remnants box in an Indian wedding-sari shop. Every item of clothing, down to their underwear, is in designer day-glo and vibrant clashing tincture. They will happily walk about in the drizzle with a pink ice-axe, lime-green gaiters, a purple, yellow and turquoise rucksack, blue and orange kagoul, red breeches and a hat with the Union Jack on it. It's one thing to be seen on the hill, but quite another to be seen and have other climbers throw rocks at you.

I, sadly, am not blameless. If there were bouncers on mountains I would have been refused entry to the crags on more occasions than I care to recall. It's the inappropriate nature of my clothing that has consistently let me down through the years. I've already revealed that I started out in a donkey jacket, but I should add that it took me at least ten years to get a decent kit. A friend knitted me a fabulous Nordic jumper, which immediately took on the status of security blanket. During heat waves, companions walked beside me in shorts and a T-shirt, while I lurched along in two tons of wool, certain in the knowledge that removing the jumper for 30 seconds would result in instant death by exposure.

My boots were three sizes too big for me, since the man in the shop had convinced me it was necessary. I know now he was just trying to make a sale and didn't have my size in stock, but since he was wearing a fleecy top and tracksuit trousers I believed him, and bought these huge leather edifices that a young married couple could quite comfortably live in and bring up a family. This meant that not only did the boots weigh more than a small car, but I was obliged to wear four pairs of socks to stop my feet moving about in them and turning my heels into chilli con carne. You should always be very careful when dealing with persuasive equipment sales people. If I'd stayed any longer with the villain who sold me those QE2 boots, I'd have walked from the shop with a case of tent pegs and a canoe.

As Christmas and birthdays brought more Gortex, my confidence grew and developed into mild snootiness about people who didn't wear the right things on the hill. I would tut at people trying to climb in wellingtons, and roll my eyes at those in jeans. Didn't they realise that mountaineering was a serious business? I certainly did; and I had the magenta bum-bag to prove it.

Of course I was due for a humiliation. A friend and I were driving in spring to Crarae gardens near Inveraray so I could salivate over the rhododendrons, but we grew tired of travelling at seven miles an hour behind clods in caravans and on reaching the Rest And Be Thankful pulled into the side to wander about at the base of Beinn an Lochain. This is an interesting mountain, previously a Munro, but had its stripes ripped off when the tables were cruelly revised with more accurate measurements. Since I was wearing posh garden visiting attire – a pair of thin striped leggings, white leather ballet pumps, a halterneck top, a cute bolero cardigan and dangly earrings – we were only planning to leave the car for some air. However, we climbed up a little way, just to get off the road. Then we thought we should nip over the next craggy bit to get a better view. But up there we could see an even nicer spot a few hundred feet above, so we scrambled up it. In no time at all we were standing on a huge patch of snow at the summit of a mountain only a few feet short of a Munro. There were some hill-walkers with ice-axes coming towards us from the other side of the hill, and I was trying to look as though I meant to come hill-walking dressed like a hairdresser's receptionist. Oh the disgrace and dishonour, not to mention the danger and stupidity.

Another piece of divine retribution for all those hours spent ticking others off came relatively recently. I interviewed Donald Watt, the leader of the Lochaber Mountain Rescue Team, and one of the things we talked about, both nodding sagely in agreement, was that people sometimes wear very stupid things on the hill. We swapped a few anecdotes about buffoons we had encountered and then went our separate ways, hands thrust deep into our respective double-thickness, Gortex, all-weather, storm-force shell outers. A few weeks later I met him in a wild part of Laggan. He was in his climbing gear, had an ice-axe, crampons, and a double-thick, Gortex, all-weather, storm-force shell outer. I was wearing a nylon fun-fur leopardskin coat, a hat with funny floppy bits for ears, pink fluorescent lipstick, and a pair of short sailing wellingtons. I am not even going to attempt to tell you why I was so attired, or guess at why fate should have made Donald and his equally well-equipped companions walk across that particular piece of wilderness at precisely the same time as me. All I can say is that I doubt I will be asked to join the Lochaber Mountain Rescue Team.

It's the fleecy top that has really revolutionised outdoor gear. Ten years ago everything had to be natural. Wool was big, not just for jumpers but for breeches. Never mind the fact they were as comfortable as wearing two fibre-glass tubes filled with iron filings, and stank like an incontinent old sheep dog when wet, they were natural wool and so considered correct.

The fleecy top was radical. Not only was it light, warm and washable, it also made grown men, previously never out of a brown jumper and khaki woollen breeches, dress for the hills in something pink and fluffy. To witness these bearded hard men suddenly zipping into pastel-coloured smocks was like watching Rome burn. But despite the laugh it has given us girlies at the expense of the hairy brigade, the material has its disadvantages. When you peel off your fleecy top from your fuschia thermal underwear, the static electricity is sufficient to heat and light Linlithgow for a week. In fact I hear that several Outward Bound schools are offering fortnight-long residential courses on the safe removal of the fleecy top. It's only £800 per person, but you must provide your own top and the school takes no responsibility for injuries.

Manufacturers, flushed with success over their pink fluffy man campaign, and greedy with the realisation that they can make hill-walkers wear anything as long as

Cutting a Dash

it's described as a technological breakthrough, are sitting in their factories dreaming up new and more ridiculous things to sell us. Hoping to make some money, I have taken the liberty of submitting an idea to several of their research and development departments, and I should warn you that a patent is pending.

Recognising that a lot of women are taking to the hills, and that they may feel a little intimidated by such a male-orientated sport, especially since they all dress in the same fluffy things as us now, I have come up with a startling new innovation. The thermal beard. The beards come in a range of attractive colours; pink to match your top, green, surfing blue, day-glo yellow and natural brown for those who desire a more rugged countenance, and once strapped on to the face with its Gortex-coated elastic strap, the beard provides the wearer with complete all-round chin exposure protection. There is also a safety beard, which has a sewn-in whistle, and ten feet of extra thermal beard material which can be unrolled from the chin and used as a survival bag. The beards were tested on a recent NASA space mission, where astronauts took ten-hour shifts putting the beards through their paces in a number of varied situations.

Walkers who already have real beards need not despair. There will be a range of thermal beard extensions which will simply clip on to or over the existing facial fur, providing the customer with that little bit of extra insulation. In addition, an anti-static spray will be for sale to allow the customer to pull his or her fleecy top over the head without first removing the beard, in complete safety. I have priced the beards and can offer them for only £237.99 plus VAT each. You can laugh. I'll bet you get one for Christmas.

(from THE FIRST FIFTY)

R.L. Stevenson (1850–1894)

'There was an Old Man of the Cape...'

There was an old man of the Cape,
Who made himself garments of crepe;
When asked 'Do they tear?'
He replied 'Here and there;
But they're perfectly splendid for shape'.

Anon

Supper Isna Ready

Roseberry to his lady says,
'My hinnie and my succour,
O shall we do the thing ye ken,
Or shall we take our supper?'
(*Fal lal, etc.*)

Wi modest face, sae fu' o' grace,
Replied the bonny lady,
'My noble lord, do as you please,
But supper isna ready'.
(*Fal lal, etc.*)

Elspeth Davie   (b. 1919)

Allergy

The new lodger glanced down briefly at the plate which had just been put in front of him and turned towards the window with a faint smile, as though acknowledging that the day was fair enough outside, even if there was something foul within.

'I can't take egg. Sorry.'

'Can't take?' Mrs Ella MacLean still kept her thumb on the oozy edge of a heap of scrambled yellow.

'No. It's an allergy.'

'It doesn't agree?'

'No. It's an allergy.'

'Oh, one of those. That's interesting! But you *could* take a lightly boiled egg, couldn't you?'

'No, it's an allergy to egg.'

'You mean *any* egg?'

'Any and every egg, Mrs MacLean. In all forms. Egg is poison to me.' Harry Veitch did not raise his voice at all, but this time his landlady withdrew the plate rather quickly. She put it on one side and sat down at the other end of the table.

'Yes, that *is* interesting,' she said. 'I've known the strawberries and the shellfish and the cat's fur. And of course I've heard of the egg, though I've never met it.' Veitch said nothing. He broke a piece of toast. 'No, I've never met it. Though I've met eggs disagreeing. I mean really disagreeing!'

Veitch was pressing his lips with a napkin. 'Not the same

Allergy

thing,' he said. 'When I say poison I mean poison. Pains. Vomiting. And I wouldn't like to say what else. Violent! Not many people understand just *how* violent!'

Flickers of curiosity alternated with prim blankness in Mrs MacLean's eyes. 'And aren't there dusts and pollens – horse's hair and that sort of thing?'

'All kinds. I don't know the lot. But they're not all as *violent.*'

There was a silence while Mrs MacLean with a soft napkin gently, gently brushed away the scratchy toast-crumbs which lay between them in the centre of the table.

'Do you find people sympathetic then?' she enquired at last.

Veitch gave a short laugh. 'Mrs MacLean – when, may I ask, have people ever been sympathetic to anything out of the ordinary?'

'I suppose that's true.'

They both turned their heads to look out onto the Edinburgh street, already crowded with people going to work. There was a stiffish breeze – visitors from the south, like Veitch, used the word 'gale' – and those going eastwards had their teeth bared against it and their eyes screwed up in a grimace which made them appear very unsympathetic indeed. On the pavement below their window, a well-dressed man stooped in the swirling dust to unwind a strip of paper which had wrapped itself round his ankle like a dirty bandage. They heard his curse even with the window shut.

This sudden glimpse of the cruelly grimacing human beings, separated from them only by glass, gave them a stronger sense of the warmth within. Human sympathy too. Mrs MacLean was a widow. It was a street of widows – some of them old and grim, living at street level between lace curtains and brown pots of creeping plants, some of them young and gay behind high window boxes where the hardiest flowers survived the Scottish summer. Mrs

Elspeth Davie

MacLean was neither of these. She was an amiable woman in her middle years, and lately she had begun to wonder whether sympathy was not her strongest point.

In the weeks that followed Veitch's status changed from lodger to paying guest, from paying guest, by a more subtle transformation shown only in Mrs MacLean's softer expression and tone of voice, to a guest who, in the long run, paid. They talked together in the mornings and evenings. Sometimes they talked about his work which was in the refrigerating business. But as often as not the conversation veered round to eggs.

As a subject the egg had everything. It was brilliantly self-contained and clean, light but meaty, delicate yet full of complex far-reaching associations – psychological, sexual, physiological, philosophical. There was almost nothing on earth that did not start off with an egg in some shape or form. And when they had discussed eggs in the abstract Veitch would tell her about all those persons who had tried their best to poison him, coming after him with their great home-made cakes rich with egg, boggy egg puddings nourishing to the death, or the stiff drifts of meringue topping custards yellow as cowslip. It was all meant kindly, no doubt, yet how could one be sure?

'You'd be amazed,' he said. 'Even persons who profess to love one aren't above mixing in the odd egg – just to test, just to make absolutely certain one isn't trying it on.'

'Oh heavens – Oh no!' cried Mrs MacLean. 'Love! Love in one hand and poison in the other!'

'That's just about it,' Veitch agreed. 'With my chemical make-up you get to know a lot about human nature, and sometimes the things you learn you'd far, far rather never have known.'

By early spring Mrs MacLean and her lodger were going out together in his car on a Saturday, sometimes to a quiet tea-room on the outskirts of the city or further out into the country where they would stretch their legs for a bit before

Allergy

having a leisurely high tea in some small hotel, where, as often as not, Mrs MacLean would inform waitress and sometimes waiters about Harry Veitch's egg allergy. Then Veitch would sit back and watch the dishes beckoned or waved away, would hear with an impassive face the detailed discussions of what had gone into the make-up of certain pies and rissoles, and would occasionally see Mrs MacLean reject a bare-faced egg outright.

He never entered into such discussions. It almost seemed as though he had let her take over the entire poisonous side of his life. On the whole, he seemed to enjoy the dining-room dramas when all heads would turn and silence fall at the sound of Mrs MacLean's voice rising above the rest: 'No, no, it's poison to him! Not at all – boiled, scrambled, poached – it's all the same. Poison!' But once in a while the merest shadow of irritation would cross his face, and on some evenings he drove home almost in silence, a petulant droop to his lips.

Before long Mrs MacLean had given up eating eggs herself. She wouldn't actually say they disagreed with her nowadays. That would be carrying it too far. But how could what was poison to him be nourishment to her? She hardly noticed when the usual invitations to suppers with neighbours began to dwindle under her too vivid descriptions of eggs and their wicked ways. She was too busy devising new, eggless dishes for Veitch. By early summer she and her guest had explored the surrounding countryside and every out-of-the-way restaurant in the city.

Mrs MacLean gave him a great deal. It was not only his stomach she tended. She gave him bit by bit, but steadily and systematically, the history of Edinburgh as they went about. 'You're standing on History!' she would exclaim, nudging him off a piece of paving-stone. Or, as he stood wedged momentarily in the archway of a close on a wild afternoon, her voice would rise triumphantly above the

Elspeth Davie

howlings and whistlings around him: 'You're breathing in History! Look at that inscription above your head!'

By late autumn Veitch had got his job well in hand. It was expanding, he said. Really bursting its bounds. Mrs MacLean knew little about his job, but she identified with it and she was not one to stand in the way of his work. When he spoke of expansion and bursting bounds, however, refrigeration was the last thing she had in mind, but rather some mature and still seductive woman bursting through all the freezing restrictions into a boundless new life. But she felt a difference. He was not so available now. He worked late and had little appetite for the original eggless dishes she set before him at supper.

Worst of all, when a few days of unexpected Indian summer began, a sudden spate of work took him away from her for longer and longer sessions. He began to be busy on Saturday afternoons, and even on Sundays he found he must use the car to make certain contacts he'd had no time for during the week. Reluctantly, Mrs Maclean decided that until the pressure of work slackened she would simply take a few bus trips on her own while the weather lasted.

She set off, good-naturedly enough, on solitary sprees at the weekends – as often as not ending up with tea alone in some country hotel or seaside café where they had been earlier in the year. She still had supper and breakfast talks with her lodger, but mostly it was herself talking to keep her spirits up. She never mentioned History now. Egg-talk was also out. In the bleak evenings she secretly yearned for the buttery omelettes and feathery soufflés she had whipped up in the old days.

One Saturday afternoon she took the bus right out into the country to an old farmhouse where they had been a couple of months ago. It stood well back from the road amongst low, gorse-covered hills, and winding through these were deep paths where you could walk for miles in

Allergy

a wide circle, eventually coming out again near the house. Mrs MacLean decided to take her walk after tea.

It was one of the last warm days of the year – so warm that after half an hour or so she had to remove her coat, and a mile further on uphill she was glad to lean on a gate and look down to where, far off, she could just see the line of the Crags and Arthur's Seat with the blue haze of the city beneath. Near at hand the weeds of the fields and ditches were a bright yellow, yet creamed here and there in the hollows with low swathes of ground-mist.

But something jerked her from her trance. She realised with a shock that she was not the only person enjoying the surroundings. Unseen, yet close to her behind the hedge, there were human rustlings and murmurings. She bent further over the gate and craned her head sideways to look. Seated on a tartan rug which came from the back of her own drawing-room sofa was Harry Veitch, his arm round the waist of a young woman whose hair was yellow as egg yolk. Their legs lay together, the toes of their shoes pointed towards one another, and Mrs MacLean noted that under a dusting of seeds and straws Veitch's shoes still bore traces of the very shine she had put there the night before.

For a few seconds longer she stood staring. From the distance of a field or two away it would have seemed to any onlooker that these three persons were peacefully enjoying the last moments of an idyllic afternoon together. Then, Mrs MacLean suddenly lifted her hands from the top of the gate as though it had been electrically wired, turned swiftly and silently down the way she had come and made for the bus route back to the city.

Sunday breakfast had always been a more prolonged affair than on other days, and the next morning Harry Veitch came downstairs late in green and white striped pyjamas under a maroon dressing-gown. He looked at ease, and on

Elspeth Davie

his forehead was a faint glow which was nothing more nor less than the beginning and end of a Scottish sunburn. For the weather had broken. Mrs MacLean greeted him, seated sideways at the table as usual to show that she had already eaten. But now Veitch was showing a strange hesitation in lowering himself into his seat. For some moments he seemed to find extraordinary difficulty in removing his gaze from the circumference of the plate before him, as though its rim were magnetic to the eyes which, try as they might to burst aside, were kept painfully riveted down dead on its centre. But at last, with tremendous effort, he managed to remove them. Casually, smiling, he looked round the room at curtains, pot-plant, firescreen, sideboard – greeting them first before he spoke. And when he spoke it was in an equable voice, polite and low-pitched.

'Mrs MacLean, I can't take egg. Sorry.'

'Can't take?' There was a cold surprise in her voice. Veitch allowed himself one darting glance at the smooth boiled egg on his plate and another at the mottled oval of his landlady's face, and again let his eyes roam easily about the room.

'No, it's an allergy,' he said.

Mrs MacLean now got up with the teapot in her hand and poured out a cup for her lodger. 'I don't quite catch your meaning, Mr Veitch,' she said, coming round and standing with the spout cocked at his ear as though she would pour the brown brew into his skull.

'An allergy, Mrs MacLean,' said Veitch, speaking with the distinct enunciation and glassy gaze of one practising his vocabulary in a foreign tongue. 'I have an allergy to egg.'

'Do you mean you want special treatment here, Mr Veitch?'

'Mrs MacLean, I am allergic to egg. Egg is poison to me. Deadly poison!'

Allergy

Mrs MacLean's face was blank, her voice flat as she answered: 'Then why should you stay here? In an egg-house.'

'An egg-house!' The vision of a monstrous six-compartment egg-box had flashed before Veitch's eyes.

'Yes, I love eggs,' she replied simply. 'Eggs are my favourite. I shall order two dozen eggs tomorrow. There will be eggs, fresh eggs, for breakfast, for lunch, for supper. Did you know there are ways of drinking eggs? One can even break an egg into the soup for extra nourishment. I have books crammed with recipes specifically for the egg. There are a thousand and one ways . . .'

'Poison!' cried Harry Veitch on a fainter note.

'Yes, indeed . . . if you stay. A thousand and one ways . . .' she agreed. And for a start – with the expression of an irate conjurer – she produced a second boiled egg out of a bowl and nimbly bowled it across the table towards her shrinking lodger.

* * *

'Doctors, like mini-cab drivers, are the other idiots to whom we trust our lives.'
James Kennaway
(1928–1968)

David Kilby   (b. 1950)

A Tale of Ordinary Love

I want tae thank you all for coming. I know Ella would be touched if she had seen the turnout here today. You'll know that I'm no' a man for the words and I don't go in for any sort of public talkin' or anything like that. I hope you've all got a drink. There's plenty of it. I've got a beer barrel in the kitchen and there's plenty of whisky. There's a bottle of malt for the minister. Your helper said you'd a taste for malt, minister. There's vodka for the ladies and even some Bacardi. Ella used to drink Bacardi and Coke, as you well know. Oh by the way, thanks for the bottle shaped wreath.

I remember she had a Bacardi and Coke in her hand when I first met her. It was in the Picardy lounge bar. It's no' in Renfield Street any more. I couldn't get over how sophisticated she looked. And her voice, dead sexy. I remember her first words to me. I saw what she was drinkin' so I thought, I'll buy her a Bacardi and Coke and just walk up to her dead cool and that. So I did. I was there in my hipster flairs and my floral shirt wi' my kipper tie. Some girls in that place couldnae take their eyes off me. There's a wee drink for you, I said. Where's the ice and lemon, ya eejit ye? says she.

What a looker she was tae. Black eye make-up and back-combed hair. Sophistication in three inch heels. She used to lacquer her hair to death. It was like tryin' tae run your fingers through a miner's helmet.

I walked her home that night and we both felt sick so we

A Tale of Ordinary Love

ran up a side street and I said, 'After you'. And she said, 'Oh, a gentleman'. Some of you older hands'll remember her from then. She was a beauty. A real stunner.

Aye, well there's some ham sandwiches. Some! There's a bloody great heap of them and I'd like to thank Betty Welsh for no' comin' to the funeral . . . No, I don't mean that like it sounded. I'd like to thank Betty Welsh for staying back and makin' the sandwiches. She told me to tell you that the pile on the right have ketchup on them and the pile on the left have brown sauce on them. So you can wire in. And I should also mention Harry Sands from the Old Log Inn for jumpin' in with a catering pack of snowballs and caramel wafers so that all you with a sweet tooth'll no' be forgotten about either.

Oh yes – and the Reverend Jack Black, thanks for some of the wonderful and touching things you said about Ella. Even though you'd never seen us before I felt as if you'd known us aw your days. And thank you for almost getting her name right, Reverend. It's MacInespie. A very brave first attempt, minister. So, enjoy your malt. Your helper said you'd aye got a good thirst for it. I think drouth was the word he used.

I've heard it said that the funeral is part of the grieving process. And I can certainly tell you that this funeral has done me a power of good. I know that Ella won't mind me sayin' that. She'll be up there now laughing her socks off. I suppose I should've gone to the Co. but Gerry said he'd got connections and he could get it cheap. And he did that. Mind you, he did warn us not to hold the coffin by the handles. I'm sure Uncle Bob's foot isn't broken. But we'll find out when he gets back from the hospital.

And wasn't it lucky that the hearse driver carries his insurance documents with him. I'm sure that being pulled on to the hard shoulder by the police gave us all more time to reflect on the solemnity of the situation. Once more we had a further opportunity to say our goodbyes

David Kilby

to Ella as the undertaker and the driver changed that baldy tyre.

Ella, as you are probably aware, hated mechanical things, so it probably came as no surprise to you that the conveyer belt taking the coffin through the curtains broke down. What can I say about our old pal, Graham Hyslop? If anyone would carry a pocket size tool kit at a funeral, I should have known that it would be Graham. To see him stripping down that conveyor belt was a real treat for those who are inclined towards the engineering arts.

And not one of his tools was longer than six inches. And him wi' that glass eye too. Surely Scottish industry could find a place for that man.

Anyway, we're all here now. Ready to have a wonderful party. It's what Ella would have wanted. A bloody good party. You remember some of the parties that've been held in this house over the years. My god, there's been some singing in this house. The bottles that have been spun in this very living room would send a rocket into orbit. The foundations must have moved a good six inches. Remember Hogmanay, when was it? About ten years ago. Ella started it in the true Scottish tradition. A chip pan fire. There we were drinkin' away and the firemen broke in the door wi' their axe and Ella said, 'Is it no' a bit early for the first foot?' The heid fireman rushed in and asked if we were all right 'cos we were all sittin' in the lounge including Ella who was cookin' the chips. 'Never mind aw right,' says Ella, 'where's the black bun and your bottle?'

Remember our wedding. It seems like only yesterday we were tucking into the roast chicken with bacon at the Old Log Inn. Harry Sands to the rescue again. He cleared a few tables and put on a great spread. It's a pity the in-laws didn't get on. I would have liked to have tasted the wedding cake before it went down the toilet.

I know it was only a City Bakeries Hallowe'en cake with

A Tale of Ordinary Love

extra icing but some of us only get married the once. Aye, okay Andy, I said some of us.

I was drunk as a monkey that day. I was in no condition to exercise my conjugal rights. So it was just as well I'd done it a wee while before. That wasn't the only reason we got married. Just because we were losers at Brig'ton roulette. Anyway we got a lovely prize wi' our son, Terry.

I can mind the first time Ella and me made love, although that's no what we called it then. I remember with tremendous clarity Ella's words as I reached for the Craven A.

'Is that it?' she said. And as far as I was aware that *was* it. It's no' like havin' a drink where you'll maybe have a wee singsong or a fish supper after. I used to wear a medallion in those days. Ella said it was like sleeping with the lord provost. But it left a green mark on her chest so she made me stop wearing it. She got tae quite like it once she got the knack of doin' it and breathin' at the same time.

Terry and Julie. Not names for children I'd've chosen, truth to be told. No, Terry, Julie, only kidding. Remember that song, 'Terry meets Julie, Waterloo sunset, every Friday night'. It was yer mammy's favourite. I suppose it's no' often the Kinks get played at a funeral.

Terry has grown up to be one of those scallywags that won't do a thing his father tells him. And why should he? What sort of example have I set over the years? Just working hard and paying for his clothes and food and everything. Lies about aw day. He gets dizzy when he's got to stand up. Ella called him 'The Horizontal Man'. The boy's twenty-one but I'm still payin' for his clothes and food and everything. Probably for his drugs as well. No, I will not shut up, son. Anyway, who do you think you're kidding? Acupuncture, my arse. Thinks we're all daft.

Remember the time when you were about six, son. And the doorbell rang and you went and answered it and you

David Kilby

came back and said, 'Mammy, there's a woman at the door wi' a fat baldy man'. And Ella said, 'It's all right, son, go back and tell the woman we've already got one'. And Julie. So beautiful, like your mammy. Dark hair, brown eyes, the cheek bones of an Egyptian cat. Julie, grown into womanhood, and looking so like your mammy. Ella, was a woman who worked. An armature balancer of some renown. There weren't many washing machines left that work without at least having had part of its engine touched by my wife. A real source of pride. Ella, a great mother and armature balancer. Till she was made redundant. They redunded a good woman that day, let me tell you.

I remember when Terry was born. I'd just been made redundant myself. The first of many. Ella said it was all right, we'd get by. We'd got a nice wee council house on a nice wee estate. And I got another job and Ella got her wean. My new job didnae pay much, so Ella went back tae work. Balancin' armatures. Ella's ma looked after Terry. And he grew up tae be a right spoilt wee . . . Well, you grew up wasted. I'm no' blamin' you. I'm no' even blamin' your granny. God rest her soul. It doesnae seem that long since she passed on. I've never seen a diabetic eat as much chocolate as she did. And no' that diabetic stuff either. The full glass and a half of sugar in every bar.

But Terry, if your mammy hadnae gone tae work then you wouldn't have turned out to be the spoilt creep you are today. Your granny gave intae your every wish. And Julie an' aw, but at least Julie tried. Julie, my darlin', turned out a real beauty.

And I'm sure you would have finished that hairdressers' course if you hadnae got yourself pregnant. It's a pity Ella will never see your wean. I know it was something that she regretted. But we cannae fault you for ambition. Who else would have thought of setting up a hairdresser's in

A Tale of Ordinary Love

the lobby press? Don't you worry, I'll see to the rewiring. I cannae help but wonder who the father is? But that was just typical of you, Julie. Generous to a fault.

I suppose it's our fault, me and Ella. Maybe if Ella hadnae worked you would have been brought up better. But we needed the money.

This wee house is goin' to seem pretty full when that wean comes. If I felt safe goin' out at night I would go for a walk to the park where Ella and me did our winchin'. I remember holding her tight, her body pressing hard against mine trying to touch her all over at once. I can feel my fingers in her hair and see such fire in her eyes. I can remember when the passion pumped through our veins till we could hardly see. Nothing else mattered in the world but my love for Ella.

Now your mammy's dead and I feel as if I've done everything wrong in my life. I made nothin' easy for her. I could give her no comfort as we struggled. We just ground our way through life until there was nothing left of either of us. We had a few laughs. We've drunk a few bottles and I did love her. I did want to do much more for her. Forty-four is no age to leave this earth. Cancer seems a feeble excuse. I don't know what else I could have done. I couldn't have worked any harder at the jobs I had. I never done anybody down.

But the nice wee council house is a slum now, and the estate is some kinna ghetto. My son'll die before I do and my daughter'll turn into a zombie. She's pregnant in a place where schoolkids run wi' drugs. Julie, who the hell's goin' to want their hair cut in our lobby press?

Anyway, everybody help yourself to a drink and a piece. If you'll excuse me, I think I'll go and get some air.

107

John McKay

The Natural History of Scotland

'Eck' is an aspiring young Scottish media type.'Willie', his father, is a deceased Hoover salesman.

WILLIE. The museum? Why've you come here?
ECK. This is where I come to think, awright?
WILLIE. Could you no have stayed doon the park and thunk? It's aw dark and dingy in here.
ECK. Aye it's dark and dingy. And that's the whole point. This is where I come to do what Scots are best at.
WILLIE. Shinty?
ECK. Moping. It's a need we've got. And we're experts. Now most folk when they're depressed, after Scotsport and that, they make do wi cryin into their last lonely can of special. But I come here to see history gummed up, life stuck on a pin. To see the elephants wi the wrinkly ears, and the dusty fish, and the big whale skeleton hanging from the roof, and sometimes, when I'm feeling really miserable, when I really want to reassure masel that life is utterly terrible, I come to the pickle room. You go up here, up through the insect's gallery, wi the Diseases Preying on Man section, and up the back stairs through the spiky crabs bit and the blown-up jellyfish, and you're here: aw the pickles in jars in glass cases, aw white and still. Brilliant. Aw the things that didnae live, hangin in jelly.

The Natural History of Scotland

Hail Caledonia! I'm fed up wi it.

(from DEAD DAD DOG)

*   *   *

'It is never difficult to distinguish between a Scotsman with a grievance and a ray of sunshine.'
P.G. Wodehouse
(1881–1975)

Eric Linklater   (1899–1974)

A Burial at Sea

The captain came towards him, and said, 'I think we've gone far enough, Mr Arbuthnot. You told me to go out beyond the Isle of May, but the weather won't get any better, and some of our passengers are not looking very well.'

Indeed, the tug was now lurching steeply, and Max, as he stood up, had again to grasp the oaken rail. He looked to the south and east, and saw grey seas rearing to ragged crests. It was nothing like gale weather – the wind was no more than fresh – but the sea was turbulent, and away to the north-east the Isle of May was hidden by a plume of white feathers as the waves broke over it. 'All right,' he said. 'We'll have the service here. Can you get the parson out? And tell someone to warn the others?'

'In just a moment,' said the captain, and telling the man at the wheel to turn her head to the wind, rang the engine-room telegraph for half-speed, then less than that, and quickly had his ship pointing to the south-east and almost stationary in the wild flux of the sea: stationary, that is, except for a violent and irregular vertical motion.

She was a large, ocean-going tug, originally chartered by Max's firm to bring home a ship that had gone ashore in the Oslo Fjord, and held for a week more, with another of the same sort, to tow a floating-dock from Grangemouth to the Clyde. She had a small well-deck between the bridge and the fo'c'sle-head, and it was there that the service was to be held. The captain, in his wisdom, had had life-lines

A Burial at Sea

made fast across it, and when the mourners emerged from shelter – half of them the colour of wet dish-cloths or winter-shrivelled cabbage leaves – many clung to the ropes with convulsive effort and a pathetic gratitude. Of the original twenty-two who had gathered for luncheon in Max's house on Corstorphine Hill, no fewer than seventeen came on deck; and none who had seen their condition could blame the remainder for staying below.

The mourners, however, even the sturdiest, presented a less dignified appearance than they had worn ashore. Most of the men had been so thoughtful as to bring tweed caps, as well as their top hats, and now, with their caps pulled fiercely down, they looked coarsely proletarian or aggressively sporting; while the women, hooded closely in scarves or mufflers, were like weather-beaten, dissipated gipsies.

Jessie, supported by Max and the captain, retained her dignity with no apparent effort; but the Rev. Mr Myrtle, whom the mate and the engineer held upright, was white as bog-cotton and limp as grass. He was a young man of resolute temper, however, and with a truly heroical contempt for physical weakness he began to recite in a loud voice the psalm *Domine, refugium*. He had got as far as the verse, 'In the morning it is green, and groweth up; but in the evening it is cut down, dried up, and withered' – when he was aware of an interruption.

Annie, whose attention had been wandering, had just seen a great wave break in wild white plumage over the distant Isle of May. She stood on the port side of the well-deck, in the shelter of the fo'c'sle-head, and nearby were Tom Murdoch and Hugh Burnett, the banker and the doctor from Peebles. Another wave broke, and rose in a prodigious high fountain above the drenched island.

'Oh, look!' she cried. 'What's that? What is it called?'

'The Isle of May,' she was told.

111

Eric Linklater

'The Isle of May? I never heard of it! Has it always been there?'

'Always.'

'And I never knew! Well, isn't that funny. What a lot you learn by going to sea.'

Mr Myrtle's attention wandered, his resolution faltered, and *Domine, refugium* came untimely to an end. A fan of spray opened above the blunt bow of the tug, and closing as it fell, revived Mr Myrtle's failing spirit with a cold salt douche. Bravely he began to read, and now in a stronger voice, 'There is one glory of the sun, and another glory of the moon, and another glory of the stars; for one star differeth from another star in glory.'

Against the clamour of the wind the Corinthian mystery was very nobly stated; but again Mr Myrtle felt his strength ebbing, and when he declared 'Man that is born of woman hath but a short time to live, and is full of misery,' it was impossible to doubt either the truth of what he said or his own conviction of it.

The captain gave an order that brought the bow of the ship from south-east to east, and Jessie, cautiously holding the urn and carefully guided by Max, took a hesitant step towards the port side, which was now the lee side. The men took off their caps, and the wind made their hair look like ludicrous wigs.

'We therefore,' said Mr Myrtle, 'commit his ashes to the deep' – and at that moment Jessie, very foolishly, took the lid off the urn to pour the remnants of old Charlie over the side. But the wind got at them first.

The wind still blew from the south-east, but about the tug there were innumerable draughts and eddies, there were counter-winds and wilful airs, and one such vagrant breeze or opposing gust scooped out the ashes, blew them about like a lunatic storm of hail, and then, in a momentary calm, let them settle, for the most part, on the wet heads and shoulders of the dispirited mourners.

A Burial at Sea

Jessie herself was unaware of the mishap – her eyes were closed, her thoughts far off – and neither Max nor Mr Myrtle, by word or movement, let her know that anything had gone wrong.

'Lord, have mercy upon us,' said Mr Myrtle, and it was with exceptional fervency that several of the mourners made the response, 'Christ, have mercy upon us.'

The service came to an end, and quickly Max took his sister back to the captain's cabin. Then he went on deck again, and in a very bad temper began to pick fragments of old Charlie from his wet coat.

On the well-deck the other mourners were all similarly engaged. They helped each other – 'Do my back and I'll do yours' – and gradually the morsels of incinerated bone were gathered together and carefully thrown overboard. Old Charlie, or the greater part of him, was eventually given the burial he had desired, but his ashes were scattered over an uncommonly wide area; for now the tug-boat was heading for home again, and making good speed.

Though deeply regretted by all there, the unfortunate conclusion of what should have been a dignified ceremony had a happy effect on those who had suffered most from the roughness of the sea: they were given something to talk about, something so unusual in its impact that it made them forget their physical unhappiness, and this, together with the comforting knowledge that they were homeward bound, let them recover their customary poise and normal spirits. The tug rolled boisterously, sending out great hissing surges from its lee side, but their voices grew louder and more confident, and long before they reached Leith they were walking the deck with the assurance of old salts, and talking of other days when all but they, and a few of the ship's officers, had succumbed to the anger of the Channel, or the Pentland Firth, or the Bay of Biscay. Even the worst of the invalids, the poor quintet that had failed

Eric Linklater

to attend the service, were revived by hearing of what had happened, and now ventured on deck to look hopefully for any scraps that might yet remain as visible evidence of the fiasco. They were encouraged in their search by Annie, who assured them that she, for one, had not been at all surprised by what had happened.

'It was just what I expected,' she said. 'Poor Charlie, he was always so clumsy.'

(from THE MERRY MUSE)

Anon

Tweed Versus Till

Says Tweed to Till
  'What gars ye rin sae still?'
Says Till to Tweed
  'Though ye rin with speed
  And I rin slaw,
  For ae man that ye droon
  I droon twa.'

Thomas Hood   (1799–1845)

Sally Simpkin's Lament, or, John Jones's Kit-Cat-Astrophe

'OH! What is that comes gliding in,
   And quite in middling haste?
It is the picture of my Jones,
   And painted to the waist.

'It is not painted to the life,
   For where's the trousers blue?
Oh, Jones, my dear!—Oh dear! my Jones,
   What is become of you?'

'Oh! Sally dear, it is too true,—
   The half that you remark
Is come to say my other half
   Is bit off by a shark!

'Oh! Sally, sharks do things by halves,
   Yet most completely do!
A bite in one place seems enough,
   But I've been bit in two.

'You know I once was all your own,
   But now a shark must share!
But let that pass – for now to you
   I'm neither here nor there.

'Alas! death has a strange divorce

Sally Simpkin's Lament

Effected in the sea,
It has divided me from you,
And even me from me.

'Don't fear my ghost will walk o' nights,
  To haunt as people say;
My ghost *can't* walk, for oh! my legs
  Are many leagues away!

'Lord! think when I am swimming round,
  And looking where the boat is,
A shark just snaps away a half
  Without a quarter's notice.

'One half is here, the other half
  Is near Columbia placed:
Oh! Sally, I have got the whole
  Atlantic for my waist.

'But now adieu – a long adieu!
  I've solved death's awful riddle,
And would say more, but I am doomed
  To break off in the middle.'

*   *   *

'This friend of mine had a terrible upbringing. When his mother lifted him up to feed him, his father rented the pram out. Then when they came into money later his mother hired a woman to push the pram – and he's been pushed for money every since! I asked him once what his ambition was and he replied it was to have an ambition. In the end tragedy struck – as he lay on his death-bed he confessed to three murders. Then he got better.'

Chic Murray
(1919–1985)

Susie Maguire (b. 1958)

Barry Norman's Tie

Have you ever heard the expression 'barry' – as in fab, brilliant, really-really-nice? Like, 'that's a barry tie'? People I know used to say it all the time, not just about ties obviously. Anyway, it just came into my mind the other day, because I was watching Barry Norman, you know, the film guy on TV, and I noticed that he had on this really quite okay tie, which is unusual for him. Because, well, a) he usually wears these horrible patterned sweaters that older men think makes them look younger, b) when he does wear a tie, it's the colour of porridge, or something to do with cricket, and c) – I can't think what I was going to say for c). A) and b) are probably enough. Oh, c) was about when he's at Cannes, at night, and it's pouring with rain, and he's wearing a velvet bow tie and shoving a microphone up Arnold Schwarzenegger's nose.

Och, anyway, there he was one night wearing this actually quite nice tie, like it didn't shout at you, you know? It was um, thingmy – discreet. It didn't get between him and what he was saying about Bruce Willis. And I was so amazed that I wrote and told him I liked his tie.

Veronica thought I was being a sap. She said I'd never get a reply, but that's only because when she sent a fan letter to Keanu Reeves, she just got this boring photograph of him and his bare chest, with a sort of laser-printed squiggle in the corner for an autograph. She tried to pretend she wasn't disappointed, like she hadn't fantasised that he'd be calling and asking her out and they'd fall-in-love-get-married-and-live-in-a-five-bedroom-house-with-a-pool-in-Malibu, or something. But I could tell, and she's been sour grapes ever since about me and Barry Norman. Because he *did* reply. On headed notepaper. He said:

Dear Marina McLoughlin,

Thank you for your very charming letter. I have many ties, and I like all of them, but I don't usually think about them, unless my wife or my producer tell me the one I'm wearing has been irrevocably stained by the product of BBC lunches. In this instance, the tie was a recent birthday present from my daughter, and I'm glad you approve!

I hope you keep watching the show,
Best wishes, Barrg Normaach.

Honestly, that's what his signature looked like it would sound like if you said it, Barrg Normaach.

Anyway, I really like the way he wrote he was glad I approved, because he could have said, 'Listen, short arse, who cares what your opinion is?' Or not replied at all.

I was dead chuffed. I watched his next programme, which was on the same night I got his letter. And the moment he came on, I thought Oh NOOOOO!! Because he was wearing the most hideous tie in the whole entire world. It was totally mingin'. It looked like something you'd buy from Oxfam for 50p to wear to a 70s night. I could hardly bear to look at him, I was so shocked – you know, when your hero turns out to have feet of lead? How could he be so incontinent?

The next day, right, I just couldn't concentrate until I wrote to him again.

Susie Maguire

Dear Barry,

Thanks a lot for your really very very interesting letter. No offence or anything though, but I watched the show last night and I thought the tie you were wearing was really – sorry – horrible. You know the one, grey with orange and green stripes, and you had on a beige shirt. Barry, you've got to do something about this.

And then I had this stupendous idea – so I added:

I've decided to make you a really brilliant tie.

Yours, etc., Marina.

And I sent it off.

Well, weeks passed, and I never got a reply, so I suppose I thought he must be offended. I watched the programme every week, plus the repeats, but he never wore the same tie twice, so I couldn't tell if maybe he'd taken my advice, or just liked the variety. Anyway, I started doing an evening course about then, in ceramics – you know, pottery? Pots?—and I got really absorbed in learning about slips and slabs and coil formations and stuff. Sounds a bit gynaecological, but it's good fun. I started making a big plate which came out really well, in the end. It's a kind of green. Nice curvy edges. I've seen things like it in galleries for pounds.

And then, out of the blue, I got a second letter from Barry Norman. It was very short.

Dear Marina,

So; where's this tie, then?

Yours, Barry Norman

Barry Norman's Tie

—only this time it looked like Brryl Normo.

Well, first I made a photocopy of the letter, and sent it to Veronica, just for cheek; and then I pinned the original to the wall beside the dressing table, so's I wouldn't forget. And every morning, when I got up, I looked at it and thought about what kind of tie would really suit him. I held up bits of fabric, and thought about his colouring; beige, taupe, grey . . . mmm, that didn't help. I kept sneaking into my dad's room and looking in his cupboard, but he's only got the one tie he got married in, that he wears for funerals, apart from the British Rail tie he wears to work, so I was totally not inspired.

Then my ceramics course ended, and I started one in Spanish, and I think the letter must have fallen down the back of the mirror one day without my noticing, because I sort of forgot about it. My mind was crammed full of thoughts like how to pronounce 'chorizo', and where to buy it. Honestly, there's all these delicatessen counters in Safeway and Tesco, but they never ever have chorizo. Was it banned or something? These german foil-wrapped twiglet things are rubbish for paella. I'm sorry, but it's chorizo or nada.

Anyway, because of my Spanish course I had to go and see this film called *Jamon, Jamon*, which is Ham, Ham, in English, in fact. I don't know if you've ever been to Spain, but in the restaurants and cafés they have these hams hanging up from the ceiling, and it's dead unhygienic, cause there are flies walking all over them for years, and then they get sliced and put on your plate. I haven't actually been myself, but Veronica's dad did and he got food poisoning and had to go home, and threw up into his souvenir straw hat during take-off. Anyway, *Jamon, Jamon*, Ham, Ham, the film, Barry Norman had recommended it actually, and it was showing in this wee cinema – the kind where there's no ice cream or popcorn, but you can drink coffee – weird – and just before the film was about to come on, before the adverts, there was a symbol up on the screen; it was a piece of celluloid, film, you know, negative film, with I think they're called sprockets, down the side, and it was sort of curling around into a big 'S' shape, as part of the film company logo. My brain sort of went 'ping'. And that's when I knew what kind of tie to make Barry Norman.

As soon as I got home, I started rummaging about in the mending cupboard. My mum was watching *NYPD Blue*, and going on about how gorgeous that guy is, the one with red hair. I have to say our tastes are quite similar actually, and I got a bit distracted when he got into the shower with no clothes on, but eventually I found what I was looking for. An old white satin nightie I used for dressing up when I was about seven and thought I wanted to be an ice-dancer, except dramatic, like Margot Fonteyn as, maybe, Lady Macbeth, on Ice. With John Curry as Banquo's ghost.

Anyway, I got the scissors and cut it up until I had a big long strip of material, and then I got out the needle and thread and sewed it up the back, so it was half the size, and turned it inside out, and then put up the ironing board, and ironed it till it looked right. Kind of like a bendy white tape-measure. Then I found this indeligible marker pen that my mum used to use for my gym things, and I started drawing, black squares and wee black dots down the side.

It was rubbish. That was the word Veronica used, and I had to agree. So, I started again, and about three days and five versions later, I got it right. It actually looked incredible, the kind of thing you'd buy in a shop, or you'd see people wearing and go 'Wow, what a barry tie.' So I packed it carefully in tissue paper, and sent it recorded delivery. And waited.

Meanwhile, back at the High Chaparral, I finally found a place that sold chorizo. They also had all kinds of other

Spanish and Mexican food, and I began to get really into it, especially the cactus salsa. Have you seen it? It's green. I wonder how they get the spines out? It's a bit scary at first, to think you're eating cactus, in case you get a spine in your throat and choke and have to go to hospital, like the Queen Mother and the fish. But it never happened. I started having cactus salsa with everything – on toast, with mince, and for a salad dressing. I got this book out the library about growing cacti and succulents – brilliant word that, succulents, makes you salivate, eh?—but eventually I realised I wasn't going to be able to grow enough prickly pears to make my own salsa unless I had a greenhouse, or I moved to Guadalajara. I even asked the guy at the hot house at the botanics, and we had this incredibly detailed conversation about mealy bug infestations and stuff, and how to grow from cuttings, and he asked me out. But that's another story . . .

Anyway, one day I came home from Spanish to find a BBC letter waiting for me. I made a cup of tea, and took it into my room, and settled down to read it – I was sure it was going to be a thank-you letter, and it was, but not quite what I'd expected.

Dear Marina McLoughlin,

Thank you for your remarkable tie. It's very clever, but you really ought to consider the personality of the person you're making it for. I never have and never would wear a bootlace tie – it's just not my style. Thanks again,

Best wishes, Brug Noord.

Honest – Brug Noord. Huh.

So. My first reaction was to feel a bit fed up. Then, really very very fed up. I thought about asking for the tie back, sending it to somebody else – but I don't think

Susie Maguire

Mariella Frostcup wears ties, she's quite feminine, and that *Moviewatch* guy is a complete banana. I didn't show the letter to Veronica, she'd just have gloated. I brooded. Yeah, I brooded. My mum was dead supportive and said she'd never liked Barry Norman anyway, and my dad just grunted something about Pearls before Swine, cause he is a bit biblical, when he's in the mood. Eventually I realised I had to write back, get it out of my system, and stop being a martyr. I took my courage in both hands and picked up my biro:

Dear Brag Noodle,

Thank you for your most interesting reply. I'm sorry you didn't like the tie. Unfortunately, my mum didn't have any brown tweed or nauseating purple and yellow stripes *in* her scraps box, so I couldn't make you the sort of tie you usually wear. Anyway, they probably wouldn't have been wide enough for you, even if she had, as she's not got anything kipper shaped.

Yours most sincerely, Marina McLoughlin.

P.S. I would continue to watch your programme if I thought you'd do something about the way you comb your hair – but who am I to comment.

And I sent it off. The next time he was on TV, I sort of watched with a different eye, you know? Like, mentally arms akimbo. He wasn't wearing my tie. He wasn't wearing a tie at all, it was one of his kiddie-on Mondrian sweater days. And he had his legs crossed, and his beige trousers sort of pulled up a bit, and you could see his fawn sock and his white leg. Euch. My Uncle Ronald always sits like that, and it put me off. And I started to notice the bags under his eyes, and the way his hand sort of *sat* there on

Barry Norman's Tie

the arm of the chair, and then twitched, just when he made one of his witty comments. And I'm afraid even that began to annoy me. A bit like Clive James – you know how he can be so funny and then suddenly you go – wait a minute, that was really nasty, why did he say that? And I started thinking about these sacred golden calves, and how they're all older men, and how we look up to them and how really they're just insecure and bitter and cynical. A bit like Burt Lancaster in that film about Hollywood with Tony Curtis em, . . . *The Strong Smell* of Something, and they're both really young and good looking? So, maybe Barry Norman and Clive James are like Burt Lancaster in the story, they've seen so much corruption in Show Biz, they wouldn't recognise a gift horse if they looked it in the mouth?

Mind you, Burt Lancaster was totally brilliant. See when he was in that other film, with the helicopter on the beach, you know, in Scotland? That one, with Peter Capaldi doing his sparey voice? He was just like he was in *Bird Man of Alcatraz*, but older: but there was no bird. They had a mermaid, though, sort of. Anyway.

You know what? I bet Burt Lancaster would have liked my tie. He would have got the point. I mean it wasn't just A Tie, was it? It was a tribute. It was a gift horse. It was the gift horse of Troy. Ha!

* * *

> '*I was standing at the bus stop the other day when a man came up to me and said, "Have you got a light, mac?" I said, "No, but I've got a dark brown overcoat."*'
> Chic Murray
> (1919–1985)

Liz Lochhead   (b. 1947)

Favourite Shade

She's getting No More Black, her.
You've got bugger all bar black, Barbra.
Black's dead drab an' all.
Ah'd never have been seen
deid in it, your age tae!
Dreich. As a shade it's draining.
Better aff
somethin tae pit a bit a colour in her cheeks, eh no?

Black. Hale wardrobe fulla black claes.
Jist hingin' therr half the time, emmty.
On the hangers, hingin.
Plus by the way a gloryhole
Chockablock with bermuda shorts, the lot.
Yella kimono, ah don't know
whit all.
Tropical prints.
Polyester everything Easy-Kerr. Bit naw, naw
that was last year, noo
she's no one to give
nothing coloured
houseroom. Black. Black.
Ah'm fed up tae the back teeth lukkin' ett her.
Feyther says the same.

Who's peyin' fur it onlywey?
Wance yir workin' weer whit yi like.

Favourite Shade

No as if yiv nothin' tae pit oan yir back.
Black!
As well oot the world as oot the fashion.

Seen a wee skirt in Miss Selfridge.
Sort of dove, it was lovely.
Would she weer it, but?
Goes: see if it was black
If it was black
it'd be brilliant.

Angela McSeveney (b. 1964)

Changing a Downie Cover

First: catch your downie.

They're big animals, sleep a lot of the time,
barely stirring as they snooze endlessly
loafing around on the beds.

But they only have to see
a clean cover—

suddenly you have six by three
of feathery incorporeality kicking and screaming
in your hands.

Wrestle them to the floor
and kneel on their necks:
you can't hurt them, no bones to break.

Pushing their head into the bag
keeps them quiet

but you're never sure
till each corner is flush inside the cover
securely buttoned shut.

They give up after that.
Pinioned in floral print polycotton
they lie back down and sleep.

Edwin Morgan   (b. 1920)

The Mummy

(*The mummy* [of Rameses II] *was met at Orly airport by Mme Saunier-Seïté.* – News item, Sept. 1976)

—May I welcome Your Majesty to Paris.

—Mm.

—I hope the flight from Cairo was reasonable.

—Mmmmm.

—We have a germ-proof room at the Museum of Man
where we trust Your Majesty will have peace and quiet.

—Unh-unh.

—I am sorry, but this is necessary.
Your Majesty's person harbours a fungus.

—Fng fng's, hn?

—Well, it is something attacking your cells.
Your Majesty is gently deteriorating
after nearly four thousand years
becalmed in masterly embalmment.
We wish to save you from the worm.

—Wrm hrm! Mgh-mgh-mgh.

—Indeed I know it must be distressing
to a pharaoh and a son of Ra,

Edwin Morgan

to the excavator of Abu Simbel
that glorious temple in the rock,
to the perfecter of Karnak hall,
to the hammer of the Hittites,
to the colossus whose colossus
raised in red granite at holy Thebes
sixteen-men-high astounds the desert
shattered, as Your Majesty in life
shattered the kingdom and oppressed the poor
with such lavish grandeur and panache,
to Rameses, to Ozymandias,
to the Louis Quatorze of the Nile,
how bitter it must be to feel
a microbe eat your camphored bands.
But we are here to help Your Majesty.
We shall encourage you to unwind.
You have many useful years ahead.

—M' n'm 'z 'zym'ndias, kng'v kngz!

—Yes yes. Well, Shelley is dead now.
He was not embalmed. He will not write
about Your Majesty again.

—T't'nkh'm'n? H'tsh'ps't?
'khn't'n? N'f'rt'ti? Mm? Mm?

—The hall of fame has many mansions.
Your Majesty may rest assured
your deeds will always be remembered.

—Youmm w'm'nn. B't'f'lll w'm'nnnn.
No w'm'nnn f'r th'zndz y'rz.

—Your Majesty, what are you doing?

—Ng! Mm. Mhm. Mm? Mm? Mmmmm.

—Your Majesty, Your Majesty! You'll break your
   stitches!

—Fng st'chez fng's wrm hrm.

—I really hate to have to use a hypodermic on a mummy, but we cannot have you strain yourself. Remember your fungus, Your Majesty.

—Fng. Zzzzzzz.

—That's right.

—Aaaaaaaaah.

Raymond Travers

In the Dock: Irvine Welsh

THE CHARGE

Irvine Welsh, it is alleged that you contrived to bestow sham credibility upon the soporific city of Edinburgh through the inane and debauched outpourings of the scummy underclass who inhabit your squalid literature, and that this pseudo-subversive excrement has irreparably damaged the reputation of the team you purport to idolise, Hibernian FC.

THE PROSECUTION

I believe it was one of the Waughs – Evelyn, Auberon or Kenny, who once averred: 'All violence is a result of repressed aesthetic desire.' How ironic, then, Mr Welsh, that your ceaseless attempts to afford dignity to that weedy specimen known as the Hibs football casual, all bumfluff and bad acne, should reflect your own poverty of aesthetic appreciation. The writer-as-wrecked-genius is a posture not unknown to the 20th century. Burroughs, Bukowski and Maurice Johnston have all belittled the honourable tradition of the novel with their lowbrow pursuits but seldom has the glorification of decadence inflicted such outrage on civilised society. It is the opinion of this court that Hibernian's descent into mind-numbing mediocrity has mirrored Irvine Welsh's literary output and the two events are inextricably linked. Let us explore the evidence.

As recently as the 1970s, Hibs were a commendable

In the Dock: Irvine Welsh

example to the rest of Scottish football. Having conceded 22 goals in the space of four cup finals, they effortlessly own the approval of opponents with their generosity of spirit. Not even the procurement of a psychedelic purple kit – inspiration for Welsh's 1994 muck, the *Acid House*, incidentally – could detract from their widespread popularity. Then, the rot set in. His follow-up, *Marabou Stork Nightmares*, was a cleverly concealed castigation of that ferocious biped, Ally Brazil, as the 1980s brought a litany of losers and public revilement to Easter Road. Towards the end of the decade, the benevolent hand of friendship was extended by Wallace Mercer, but stubbornness prevailed and Hibernian refused this magnanimous gesture by neighbours, Hearts. Mr Mercer, a revered and unselfish man with the interests of the community always close to his heart, was sufficiently incensed to donate Andy Watson to Hibs by way of chastisement.

As Irvine Welsh's amphetamine-fuelled clamour for notoriety gained ground, Hibs' fortunes plummeted even further and another objectionable characteristic of the accused's personality reared its unsightly head: Namely, a near-psychopathic envy of Glasgow, dubbed 'Wegie-baiting'. I conclude that it is incumbent upon the jury to register their disapproval of this jumped-up property speculator in no uncertain manner.

CASE FOR THE DEFENCE

This tribunal considers your plea of insanity to be fallacious and suggests that supporting Hibs is not responsible for any mental disorders you claim to possess.

VERDICT

Devoid of chemical stimulation, you shall immediately be installed as writer-in-residence for *Take The High Road*,

Raymond Travers

whereby your dramatic output will concern itself with cream teas and wholesome chat. As additional punishment, you shall be furnished with a season ticket for Easter Road and forced to commute from your yuppified lodgings in suburban Amsterdam every fortnight to witness the crud currently masquerading as entertainment at that benighted club. Take him down.

Irvine Welsh   (b. 1957)

Where the Debris Meets the Sea

The house in Santa Monica sat tastefully back from Palisades Beach Road, the town's bustling ocean boulevard. This was the top end of the town, its opulence serving as the height to aspire to for the yuppie dwellers of the condominiums further down the Pacific coast. It was a two-floored Spanish-style dwelling, partly obscured from the road by a huge stone wall and a range of indigenous American and imported trees. A few yards inside the wall, an electrified security fence ran around the perimeter of the property. Inside the gate at the entrance to the grounds, a portable cabin was discreetly tucked, and outside it sat a burly guard with mirror-lens shades.

Wealth was certainly the overall impression given by the property. Unlike nearby Beverly Hills, however, the concept of wealth here seemed more utilitarian, rather than concerned with status. The impression was that wealth was here to be consumed, rather than flaunted ostentatiously for the purpose of inducing respect, awe or envy.

The pool at the back of the house had been drained; this was not a home that was occupied all the year round. Inside, the house was expensively furnished, yet in a stark, practical style.

Four women relaxed in a large room which led, through patio doors, to the dry pool. They were at ease, lounging around silently. The only sounds came from the television, which one of them was watching, and the soft hissing of the air-conditioning which pumped cool, dry air into the house.

A pile of glossy magazines lay on a large black coffee table. They bore such titles as *Wide-o*, *Scheme Scene* and *Bevvy Merchants*. Madonna flicked idly through the magazine called *Radge*, coming to an abrupt halt as her eyes feasted on the pallid figure of Deek Prentice, resplendent in a purple, aqua and black shell-suit.

'Phoah! Ah'd shag the erse oafay that anywey,' she lustily exclaimed, breaking the silence, and thrusting the picture under Kylie Minogue's nose.

Kylie inspected the image clinically, 'Hmm . . . ah dunno . . . No bad erse oan it like, bit ah'm no really intae flat-toaps. Still, ah widnae kick it oot ay bed, likesay, ken?'

'Whae's that?' Victoria Principal asked, filing her nails as she reclined on the couch.

'Deek Prentice fi Gilmerton. Used tae be in the casuals, bit eh's no intae that anymair,' Madonna said, popping a piece of chewing-gum into her mouth.

Victoria was enthusiastic. 'Total fuckin ride. Ah bet eh's hung like a hoarse. Like that photae ah goat ay Tam McKenzie, ken fi the Young Leith Team, original seventies line-up. Fuckin welt oan it, man, ah'm telling ye. Phoah, ya cunt ye! Even through the shell-suit, ye kin see ehs tackle bulgin oot. Ah thoat, fuck me, ah'd gie ma eye teeth tae get ma gums aroond that.'

'Ye'd probably huv tae, if ehzis big is ye say!' smirked Kylie. They all laughed loudly, except Kim Basinger, who sat curled up in a chair watching the television.

'Wishful thinkin gits ye naewhaire,' she mused. Kim was studying the sensual image of Dode Chalmers; bold shaved head, Castlemaine XXXX t-shirt and Levis. Although Rocky, his faithful American pit-bull terrier was not visible on the screen, Kim noted that his leather and chain leash was

Where the Debris Meets the Sea

bound around Dode's strong, tattooed arm. The eroticism of the image was intense. She wished that she'd videotaped this programme.

The camera swung over to Rocky, whom Dode described to the interviewer as: 'My one faithful friend in life. We have an uncanny telepathy which goes beyond the archetypal man-beast relationship . . . in a real sense Rocky is an extension of myself.'

Kim found this a bit pretentious. Certainly, there was little doubt that Rocky was an integral part of the Dode Chalmers legend. They went everywhere together. Kim cynically wondered, however, just how much of this was a dubious gimmick, manufactured, perhaps, by public relations people.

'Fuck . . .' gasped Kylie, open mouthed, '. . . what ah'd gie tae be in that dug's position now. Wearin a collar, chained tae Dode's airm. That wid dae me fine.'

'Some fuckin chance,' Kim laughed, more derisively than she'd intended.

Madonna looked across at her. 'Awright then, smart cunt. Dinnae you be sae fuckin smug,' she said challengingly.

'Aye Kim, dinnae tell ays ye widnae git intae his keks if ye hud the chance,' Victoria sneered.

'That's whit ah sais, bit. Ah'm no gaunny git the chance, so whit good's it talkin aboot it, likesay? Ah'm here in Southern California 'n Dode's ower in fuckin Leith.'

They fell into a silence, and watched Dode being interviewed on *The Jimmy McGilvary Show*. Kim thought that McGilvary was a pain in the arse, who seemed to feel that he was as big a star as his guests. He was asking Dode about his love-life.

'In all honesty, I don't have time for heavy relationships at the moment. Right now I'm only interested in all the overtime I can get. After all, one has to remember that trades fortnight isn't that far away,' Dode explained, slightly flushed, his thin mouth almost curling in a smile.

'Ah'd cowp it,' Kylie licked her bottom lip.
'In a fuckin minute,' Victoria nodded severely, eyes widened.
Madonna was more interested in Deek Prentice. She turned her attention back to the article and continued reading. She was hoping to read something about Deek's split from the casuals. The full story had not come out about that one, and it would be interesting to hear Deek's side of things.

There is hope for us all yet, as Deek is keeping an open mind on romance since his much publicised split with sexy cinema usherette, Sandra Riley. It's obviously an issue where Deek is keen to set the record straight.

'I suppose, in a way, we loved each other too much. There's certainly no hard feelings or bitterness on either side. In fact, I was talking to Sandra on the phone only the other night, so we're still the best of friends. Our respective careers made it difficult to see as much of each other as we would have liked. Obviously cinema isn't a nine-to-five thing, and furniture removals can take me all over the country, with overnight stays. We got used to not being together, and sort of drifted apart. Unfortunately, it's the nature of the business we're in. Relationships are difficult to sustain.'

Deek's social life is another area where he feels that he has had more than his share of unwelcome publicity. While he makes no secret of an enjoyment of the high life, he feels that 'certain parties' have somewhat exaggerated things.

'So I enjoy the odd game of pool with Dode Chalmers and Cha Telfer. All I can say is: guilty as charged. Yes, I'm in the habit of visiting places like the Spey Lounge, Swanneys and the Clan Tavern; and I enjoy a few pints of lager. However, the public only see the glamorous side. It's not as if I'm swilling away every night. Most evenings

Where the Debris Meets the Sea

I'm home, watching Coronation Street *and* East Enders. *Just to illustrate how the press get hold of nonsense, a report appeared in a Sunday newspaper, which shall be nameless, stating that I was involved in an alteration at a stag night in Fox's Bar. It's not a boozer I use, and in any case I was working overtime that night! If I was in the pub as often as certain gossip columnists claim, I'd hardly be able to hold down my driving job with Northern Removals. With three million people unemployed, I've certainly no intention of resting on my laurels.'*

Deek's boss, the experienced supervisor Rab Logan, agrees. Rab probably knows Deek better than anyone in the business, and Deek unreservedly credits the dour Leither with saving his career. Rab told us: 'Deek came to us with a reputation for being, should we say, somewhat difficult. He's very much an individual, rather than a team man, and tended to go off to the pub whenever it took his fancy. Obviously, with a flit to complete, this lack of application caused some bad feeling with the rest of the team. We crossed swords for the first and last time, and since then, Deek's been a joy to work with. I can't speak highly enough of him.'

Deek is only too willing to acknowledge his debt to the removal Svengali.

'*I owe it all to Rab. He took me aside and told me that I had what it took to make it in the removals game. The choice was mine. At the time I was arrogant, and nobody could tell me anything. However, I remember that exceptionally grim and lonely journey home on the number six bus that day Rab told me a few home truths. He has a habit of stating the transparently obvious, when you're so close to it, you can't see the woods for the trees. After a dressing-down from Rab Logan, one tends*

Irvine Welsh

to shape up. The lesson I learned from Rab that day was an important one. In a sense, the removal business is like any other. The bottom line is, you're only as good as your last flit.'

What Deek eventually wants however, is the opportunity to

'Thir's nought tae stoap us gaun tae Leith, fir a hoaliday n that,' Victoria suggested, tearing Madonna's attention from the magazine.

'Hoaliday . . . hoaliday . . .' Madonna sang.

'Aye! We could go tae the *Clan*,' Kylie enthused. 'Imagine the cock in thair. Comin oot the fuckin waws.' She screwed up her eyes, puckered her lips and blew hard, shaking her head from side to side.

'Ye'd nivir git served in thair,' Kim sniffed.

'Ken your problem, Kim? Ye nivir think fuckin positively enough. We've goat the poppy. Dinnae you sit thair n tell ays ye've no goat the hireys,' Madonna remonstrated.

'Ah nivir sais that. It's no jist aboot poppy . . .'

'Well then. We could go tae Leith. Huv a fuckin barry time. Hoaliday ay a lifetime,' Madonna told her, then continued her singing. 'It wid be, it wid be so nice, hoaliday . . .'

Victoria and Kylie nodded enthusiastically in agreement. Kim looked unconvinced.

'You cunts crack ays up.' She shook her head. 'No fuckin real.'

'Whit's wrong wi your fuckin pus, ya stroppy cunt?' Madonna mouthed belligerently, sitting up in the chair. 'Ye git oan ma fuckin tits, Kim, so ye do.'

'We'll nivir go tae fuckin Leith!' Kim said, in a tone of scornful dismissal. 'Yous ur fuckin dreamin.'

'We might go one time!' said Kylie, with just a hint

of desperation in her voice. The others nodded in agreement.

But in their heart of hearts, they knew that Kim was right.

Leonard Maguire (b. 1924)

A Literary Football Match

... and today Scotland fielded the strongest team we've seen for many years.

In the goalmouth, the man himself, Harry Mackenzie, The Man of Feeling. The back line: Blind Harry of Elderslie Athletic and Tobias Smollet, Vale of Leven, who came onto the pitch this afternoon wearing the boots he borrowed from Miguel Cervantes of Real Madrid.

Then the brilliant but ageing midfield trio – Bob Henryson of Dunfermline Aesthetic, Willie Dunbar of Berwick Rovers and, from the 2nd division, Willie Drummond who plays for Hawthornden.

The two wingers, Alex Selkirk and Davy Hume, with a lot of experience behind them; then the combined talents of Thomas Muir of Huntershill and Andy Fletcher of Saltoun, together with Scotland's international striker, Tommy Urqhuart of Cromarty!

Even before this match began it was obvious it was going to be an unusual game. The trouble started shortly after His Grace the Duke of Cumberland had shaken hands with both teams. The referee, George, er – the Third?—was just about to spin the coin when Tommy Urqhuart called him aside to propose some honourable motions and was immediately removed by the police. And so Scotland began the game with ten men!

And right away, within the first few seconds, England went ahead. Rightwinger Sammy Johnson came up with a great piledriver of a dictionary, which struck the crossbar

A Literary Football Match

and was deflected into the net, putting England into an early lead.

But Scotland were never very far behind, for almost immediately Davy Hume came back with a blockbuster, a history in six volumes, giving the goalkeeper no chance whatever, even from thirty yards out. And that made it: Scotland 1, England 1.

And Scotland back in the game once more. But England's dangerman, Johnson, who had been hugging the touchline, made a quick detour round the Highlands and declared there wasn't a tree in the whole country – 'Not enough timber, Sir, to make me a walking stick' – oh, definitely offside! A shrewd blow to Scotland here, just when the game had been going so well for them. And so the score is Scotland 1, England 2.

But then came the error for which I'm sure Johnson will never forgive himself. A sustained Scottish attack brought Johnson back defending the English goal. And, in a crude tackle upon his opponent, Tommy Muir, who is expecting a transfer from Huntershill, Johnson struck him down with a blow from his American pamphlet entitled 'Taxation No Tyranny' right in front of the goal! And it's well known that this broadside was one of the causes of the American War of Independence, and yes!—the linesman's flag is up, and the refereee has no hezzytation in placing the ball on the spot . . . and it's a gawl! And as the whistle goes for half time, it's Scotland 2, England 2.

In the second half Johnson didn't come out of the players' dressing room, and was replaced on the field by Tommy Percy of Northumberland, the author of *The Reliques of English Poetry*.

During a quiet spell in the game, winger Davy Hume apparently made a remark about the Earl of Northumberland being a shrewd boy when it came to handing over the housekeeping money. Tommy Percy naturally took

143

exception to this, and the referee moved in to separate the two players.

But Hume wasn't finished yet, for he came back with Scotland's final reply, a three-paragraph banana-shot which carried the goalkeeper, the two full-backs, Tommy Percy and the Earl of Northumberland through the back of the net! And it's all over! It's all over! There's the final whistle!

And there's a delighted crowd running on to the pitch – it's been the best day for Scotland since Bannockburn!!

* * *

'As far as I'm concerned, Scotland will be reborn when the last minister is strangled with the last copy of the Sunday Post.'
Tom Nairn
(b. 1932)

Anon

The Ways and Wiles o' Oor Wullie

Fair fa' your rosy-cheekit face,
Your muckle buits, wi' broken lace,
Although you're always in disgrace,
   An' get your spanks,
In all our hearts ye have your place—
   Despite your pranks.

Your towsy heid, your dungarees,
Your wee snub nose, your dirty knees,
Your knack o' seeming tae displease
   Your Ma an' Pa.
We dinna care a tuppenny sneeze—
   We think you're braw.

You're wee, an' nae twa ways aboot it,
You're wise, wi' very few tae doot it,
You're wild, there's nane that wad dispute it,
   Around the toon.
But maist o a'ye are reputit—
   A lauchin' loon.

Weel-kent, weel-liked, you're aye the same,
Tae Scots abroad and Scots at hame.
North, south, east, west, your weel-won fame
   Shall never sully.
We'll aye salute that couthie name—
   Oor Wullie.

          (from the 1954 OOR WULLIE ANNUAL)

James Cameron (1911–1985)

Cover Story

My days were spent in the service of the Thomson Publications, then as now a patriarchal firm of significance in its own peculiar sphere, pre-eminent of its kind in the mass-production of an especially marketable type of sub-literature, of a strangely durable but ever-changing variety. Most of this quite considerable empire was divided into two fields, on the one hand Woman's and on the other Boys'. The Women's section was presided over by Mr David Donald, the Boy's by Mr Robert Low. Both of them were to become generous and helpful friends, and introduced me to the pastime of Scottish mountaineering that became, and remained for many years, an obsessive occupation. In the office they were both very important men, while any position of less importance than mine had yet to be devised. Mr Low had under his wing the great organs of contemporary derring-do, the *Wizard*, the *Rover*, the *Hotspur*, and the like, all differing in fashions immediately perceptible to the initiate but to nobody else. Mr Donald was overlord of the *Weekly Welcome*, the *Red Letter* and the *Red Star Weekly*, each of which specialized – again in nuances not readily to be understood – in serial fiction of a nature which even after all these years I remember as either unbearably sweet and wholesome, or diabolically blood-thirsty. I was attached to the *Red Star Weekly*, which catered for a public of working girls whose tastes must have verged on the sadistic, so heavily were our pages soaked in gore. We had some sort of a lien on that hardy classic of

Cover Story

Victorian violence, *Maria Marten, or the Murders in the Red Barn*. It seems to me that we were recounting that piece of durable *angst* for years, and when it stopped the intervals were filled with sequels, or developments, or associated crimes of passion; I am not sure that we did not have a *Son of Maria Marten*. These works were contributed by sundry authors over the country, my father among them, who were paid thirty shillings a thousand words for their not inconsiderable pains.

The memorable quality of these stories was, paradoxically, their purity. The most frightful things were encouraged to happen: stranglings, knifings, shootings, disembowellings, burials alive, hauntings, drownings, suffocations, torments of a rich and varied nature abounded, and each instalment was obliged to end with a suspenseful promise of worse to come, but in no circumstances and at no point was permitted even the hint of sexual impropriety. This was the ark of the covenant and the cornerstone of our editorial principles. No matter what ferocious indignities, disasters and deaths befell our heroines, it might never be even suggested, however obliquely, that there was ever any purpose behind these excesses other than good clean violence. This made much of the carryings-on somewhat inexplicable, but that was incidental and held to be no difficulty.

This curious attitude can be symbolized in the case of the Cover Picture. One of the functions that fell to my lot was the weekly selection of some particularly gripping or galvanic incident in our principal story that could be illustrated in a compelling way and used as the magazine's cover, as an earnest of the savours within. On one occasion we were beginning a serial based on an actual series of especially brutal murders that had much exercised the newspapers of the time, and which had been catalogued in the press as 'The Man With the Glaring Eyes'. No subject was more tailor-made for us, and with eager professional zeal and pride we

147

James Cameron

had commissioned a fictionalized version of this rewarding series of crimes. In the real-life version the trouble had manifestly been caused by some unusually over-stimulated-sexual psychopath; no such innuendo, however, was to be found in our version, in which a recurrent number of nubile virgins were vigorously done to death by some antisocial unknown apparently in pursuit of a wholly mysterious hobby.

On this occasion, then, I ordered from the artist what I felt to be an appropriate drawing that would do justice to our promising theme. When the rough appeared I was well satisfied: it portrayed a deeply sinister back-alley by night, lit only by the baleful gleam of an eerie street lamp, whose sickly beam threw into prominence a foreground of damp and lowering paving-stones, on which lay the true purpose of the composition: the body of a young woman, her throat most palpably cut from ear to ear. It was a highly successful realization; the draughtsman had clearly put his heart into his work, and he had delineated the character of the lady's injury with an almost clinical fidelity; hardly was a torn tendon or a severed blood-vessel out of place, and the blood that streamed into the rainswept gutter had been limned by an enthusiast. It did complete justice, I felt, to 'The Man With the Glaring Eyes'.

I took this along for Mr Donald's approval with a quiet and calm confidence. When he saw it he blenched. He tore it from my hand and studied it aghast, and in speechless outrage. Finally he said: 'You must be mad!'

Accepting that I might possibly on this occasion have overdone it, I murmured: 'It is a bit strong, maybe.'

'Strong, strong,' cried Mr Donald. 'It's no' a question o' strong; it's no' a bad scene. But for God's sake, boy – look at the lassie's skirt; it's awa' above her knees!'

Abashed, I realized what rule I had broken. I took the drawing back and had the hemline lowered a modest inch or two, and in the cover went, slit windpipe and all.

(from POINT OF DEPARTURE)

W.N. Herbert

Why the Elgin Marbles Must Be Returned to Elgin

Because they are large, round and bluey,
　　and would look good on the top of Lady Hill.
Because their glassy depths would give local kids
　　the impression that they are looking at
　　the Earth from outer space.
Several Earths in fact, which encourages humility
　　and a sense of relativity.
Because local building contractors would use
　　JCBs to play giant games in Cooper Park
　　and attract more tourists to Morayshire:
　　'Monster Marble Showdown Time!'
Because the prophecy omitted from the Scottish Play
　　must be fulfilled:
　　'When the marbles come back to Elgin
　　the *mormaer* will rise again.'
(A *mormaer* being a Pictish sub-king.
Which Macbeth was, not a thane.
Nor a tyrant, for that matter.
More sort of an Arthur figure, you know,
　　got drunk and married Liza Minelli, with
　　Gielgud as Merlin the butler.)
Because they're just gathering dust
　　sitting in the British Museum, never mind
　　the danger that if someone leans against them
　　they might roll and squash a tourist like a bug.

W.N. Herbert

Because the Greeks, like the rest of Europe,
  don't know where Scotland is, and so
  won't be able to find them.
Because if they come looking we can just
  push the marbles into the Firth off Burghead
  and show them the dolphins instead.
Greeks like dolphins. Always have.
Because it will entertain the dolphins
  watching the Elgin marbles roll with the tides
  and perhaps attract whales.
Because whales can balance the marbles
  on the tops of their spouts,
  then ex-Soviet tourist navies can come
  and fire big guns at them
  like in a funfair.
Because the people of Morayshire were
  originally Greek anyway, as proven by
  Sir Thomas Urquhart in his *Pantochronochanon*.
And by the fact they like dolphins.
Because we are not just asking for them,
  we demand their return, and this
  may be the marble that sets the heather
  alight, so to speak.
Because if the Stone of Destiny is
  the MacGraeae's tooth, then
  the Elgin marbles are
  the weird sisters' glass eyes.
Because Scotland must see visions again,
  even if only through
  a marble of convenience.

James Robertson (b. 1958)

Sympathy for the De'il

Ma name is Lucifer. Ma mither gied it me. She thocht it had a ring tae it. I wud need tae be the only wean in the warld named for the Deil by the only mither in the warld that niver kent it. Feck o weans in Spain an Mexico an whauriver cried Jesus. I bet there's nane cried Lucifer.

Ye'd hae thocht somebody micht hae tellt her, brung it up casual like in the conversation as they dandled me on their knee – 'Lucifer nou, that's no verra nice, no verra nice at aa cryin a puir wee wean Lucifer.' But naebody did, or gin they did she didna pey ony heed, which is the mair liker. An ma faither – whaeiver he wis – wisna there tae pit her richt either; he'd pit her wrang nine month afore an hadna been seen syne. I niver did fin oot onythin aboot ma faither. She wudna speik aboot him. She wis thrawn that wey. In spite o aa ma speirins I micht as weill hae been an immaculate conception for aa that ony man had appearinly onythin tae dae wi ma bein on the yirth. In fact, there wis a spell when I uised tae wauk ivery mornin in a cauld sweit an had tae check ablow the bed-claes that I hadna grown cloots in the nicht. It had entered ma heid that if I hadna a *human* faither mibbe there wis a faimly reason why ma name wis Lucifer.

If she'd wantit tae cry me efter the Deil she cud hae dune it athout drawin attention tae the fact. There a hantle guid Scotch Christian names for Satan an naebody wud hae been ony the wiser. Whit's wrang wi Nick, say; or Sim, or Bobbie, or Sandy? Na, the truth wis, ma mither juist didna ken ony better. She'd heard the name Lucifer somewhaur – God kens whaur – an fancied it. Syne I cam alang an bure the gree.

It wisna ower lang afore I fun oot that ma haunle had certain concatenations. Ma first teacher wudna believe me when I tellt her. If they hadna abolished the belt I wud hae haen it at five year auld juist for statin ma name. She niver did manage tae caa me Lucifer straucht oot. It wis ayewis 'Luke' or 'you' – or 'Luik, you!' – or she wud juist pynt me wi her finger. Still, that wis better nor the treatment I had oot in the yairds at the big schuil frae ma fellow wee democratic intellecks. They uised tae staun roun me in a muckle circle daein spune-gabbit imitations o Mick Jagger an chantin, 'Pleased to meet you, hope you guess my name.' It was murther.

Wan day I cums hame an says tae ma mither, 'Ma, are we Proatustants or Kafflicks.' (I wis juist a wean.)

She luiks at me in a funny kinna wey. 'How?' she says. 'Has onybody at the schuil been at ye?'

'Na,' I says. 'Weill, ay. The ither laddies, they keep ettlin tae win it oot o me, an it's gey embarrasin no even kennin.'

She dichtit her hauns on her peenie an sat doun. 'Weill,' she says, 'as ye ken, I'm no really yin for religion. Yer grannie nou, she uised tae gang tae the kirk reglar as clockwark. Or the chaipel wis it? I canna mind. Onywey she dishauntit whichiver it wis efter yer granda fell in the furnace an wis brunt tae an aizle.' (Ma granda wis a gaffer in the Chalmers Lane foondry when it wis still warkin.) 'She juist fell awa efter that.'

'But Ma,' I says, 'thir laddies are speirin at me, "a Billy or a Dan or an auld tin can?", an I'm feart whit'll happen gin I get it wrang.' I didna tell her I'd only managed tae survive this faur by peyin them aff wi aa the sweeties I cud

Sympathy for the De'il

steal frae the corner shop. 'I've tae gie them ma answer the morn's morn.'

She pensed on this for a while. 'Weill, is it Protestants or Catholics that are at ye?'

I didna richt ken. Tae be honest, I didna think hauf o the wee terrorists were ower shair either, but I wisna aboot tae caa their bluff. 'Baith,' I says.

Ma mither clapped ma shouther an saftened her vyce. 'Weill, son,' she says, 'juist say ye're an auld tin can. That wey ye winna offend onybody.'

But as I fun oot tae ma cost, an auld tin can is for kickin. It wis a nae-win situation but.

Somethin aboot ma granda I mind: he wis a man o principle. (This wis afore he wis luntit.) He had the maist rigid rules tae his life. Sic as: Dinna Eat Fush on a Monday; Nae Frien Like the Penny; Niver Trust a Campbell. Weill, there wis reason in it efter aa: the fush had likely lain in the shop sin Saturday, twal pennies made up a fou shillin, an as for the Campbells, weill, hadna they slauchtered innocent fowk in their beds hardly three hunner year syne? I mind anither o ma granda's saws wis, Dinna Play Wi Fire. Muckle guid it did him.

Wheniver I wisna wi ma mither, I wud dock ma name tae Lou. But she wudna hae it, an I wis ayewis Lucifer in her een. It cud be awfu stupit, me playin fitba oot in the street wi the ither lads, an syne oor windae wud open an she'd be hingin oot o it shoutin, 'Lucifer, cum in for yer tea this minute!' An there wis the time she had tae gae in tae see the heidmaister when I'd played the kip yince ower aften, an I wis in there wi her, an ye cud tell it juist didna wash wi the heidie when she said, 'Oh, Mr McManus, I dinna unnerstaun it. Lucifer's sic a wee angel at hame.'

Na, ma mither wisna yin for religion. Anither time I

mind, I had juist stertit ma first job, stackin shelves in a supermercat, an it wis a public holiday, which juist happened tae coincide wi thon English holiday, Easter Monday. So there we were, ma mither an me, sittin in the front windae wi a cup o tea aboot three in the efternune, luikin oot at the holiday rain dingin doun, an she says tae me:

'Son, whit happens on Easter Monday?'

'Naethin,' I says. 'It's a holiday, Ma. Naethin happens.'

'Na,' she says, 'I mean, whit is it? Whit happens in the Bible on Easter Monday?' (She lippened on ma guid Scotch eddication tae pit her mind at ease on sic maitters – no that she wis aften fashed wi them.)

I thocht aboot it for a minute. 'Dinna ken,' I says. 'Easter Sunday the stane wis rowed awa an Jesus ris frae the deid. On the Monday I think he juist daunert aboot, meetin fowk an that.'

Ma mither souked that in wi her tea, syne she shuik her heid at the weather ootby. 'Weill,' she says, 'he'll no be oot the-day.'

Whit ma mither *wis* intae, wis Country an Western music. She uised tae gang aboot the house singin 'Jolene, Jolene' an 'Stand By Your Man' an aa that shite. Mibbe she thocht if she sang it aften eneuch it wud mak up for him no haein stude by her. I hatit thae sangs, but I ayewis had a hope that a C & W moral wud lie ahint ma name, an that when I raxed tae be a man ma mither on her daith-bed wud whusper in ma lug:

> Son, I ken ye hate that haunle
> An it disna haud a caunle
> Tae Tam or Shug or ony ither name;
> An tho I wudna relish
> Tae hear ye say it's hellish
> If ye canna thole it I'm the yin tae blame.

Sympathy for the De'il

This life is cruel an sair
An fowk can be unfair
An I kent I wudna aye be at yer side;
So I cried ye efter Satan
Sae ye'd lairn tae tak the hatin
An yer sel-restraint wud be a mither's pride.

O Lucifer, if Lucifer
Is no the name that you prefer,
I cud hae cried ye Mephistopheles;
But if ye want me tae be truthfu
I think that's an awfy moothfu
Whereas Lucifer trips aff the tung wi ease.

So ye see it's no unceevil
Tae be named efter the Deevil,
In fact it is the heichest from o flattery;
An as if that's no eneuch
It makes ye unco teuch
An able tae wi-staun assault an battery.

Nou don't miscaa yer mither
For ye'll niver get anither—
There's thousans wud be gratefu for yer moniker;
Ye mey think yer Ma's a daftie
But she's no, she's geyan crafty
An forby she plays a really mean harmonica.

But it niver warked oot like that. When ma mither wis dwynin awa in the hospice wi cancer o the sentiment, she tuik ma haun in hers an says tae me: 'Lucifer, I ken ye aften cry yersel Lou, but I wiss ye wud uise the haill thing. For ma sake. It souns awfu graun, dae ye no think? Lucifer! Like the name o a man that'll rise in the warld!'
    An I didna hae the hert tae disherish her o that notion.

155

Donald Gordon

Wee Jaikie's Sang

Strippit ba's is **hard tae bate,**
    Strippit ba's is really dandy.
Strippit ba's is simply great,
    Better nor yir common **candy.**
    Chocolate bars will melt awa,
Like the snowflakes i' the river.
Jericho will **surely fa:**
    Strippit ba's gie lasting pleasure
Tweedledum and **tweedledee,**
    Tap o Noth and tapsalteerie!
Fan aa ither comforts flee,
    Strippit ba's will keep ye cheery
    Babylon is blawn awa,
Egypt's host is **sairly drookit!**
Ither **sweeties** ye can chaw,
    Strippit ba's maun aye be sookit
London brig is **tummel't** doon,
    Glesca's coupit i' the river.
Embro's shoogly i' the **foun:**
    Strippit ba's will last for ivver.

    *   *   *

'I can't speak for women but I find Mikhail Gorbachev attractive as a man's man. It's an extraordinary combination of intelligence, baldness and serenity.'
                                   Sean Connery
                                      (b. 1930)

Tom Morton (b. 1955)

Bodily Functions

The rain was once more battering lumps out of the tarmac as I left Fort William. The orange beast's steering had apparently worked itself into a less shoulder-wrenching condition, and as both top and bottom nuts seemed tight, I was tentatively confident about getting to Oban, a place I had not visited since the great Ledaig toilet disaster of 1969, in one piece.

In fact, it's barely forty-five miles from Fort William to Oban, along a road made slick with the burnt-off rubber of a million tourists. Once over the Ballachulish Bridge and heading down the Argyll coastline, the primitive rawness of the northern Highlands seems a world away . . .

When I was a child, this was our holiday territory, courtesy of the Sprite Musketeer caravan my father had bought. We caravanned for years, even towing the sixteen-foot box all the way to the Costa Brava on one occasion. The continual claustrophobia of three children and two adults being crammed into that space every holiday night has left me with an absolute detestation of caravans in every shape and form.

But I remember trips north from Ayrshire, crossing the Clyde by the Erskine Ferry long before the bridge was built, then the Ballachulish ferry to head further into the Highlands. Oban was another favourite destination, although we usually stayed at the North Ledaig caravan site, over the Connel Bridge which still spans the spectacular Falls of Lora.

And there it was. Ledaig Caravan Site, much enlarged since the day of the great toilet disaster more than twenty years previously. I was a pre-adolescent, tall and gangly and sullen and hating, hating more than anything, being in a caravan over Easter with my parents and two sisters. Unfortunately, because I was also a born-again Christian, my pubescent rage at life, the universe and everything included massive dollops of guilt at feeling that way. I prayed for forgiveness and to feel better, and to love everybody.

I had, in fact, gone down to the Ledaig shore to pray, and to stop myself hammering my sisters, when the need to find a toilet became paramount. My guts went into that uncontrollable, washing-machine-on-final-rinse spasm which brooked no argument. I broke into a trot, aiming for the caravan site's toilet block.

Now my prayers had become simple, precise: God, get me to the toilet in time and I'll do anything, even accompany my father on his Sunday afternoon door-to-door evangelisation missions. I will have, as the preachers demand, a passion for souls. I will stop listening to Rolling Stones records on the radio. I also began running as fast I could without provoking disaster.

I reached the toilet block. I threw open a cubicle door. 'Thanks, God,' I breathed, silently. And that brief hesitation proved my undoing.

Well, my father found me eventually, just before he called out the mountain-rescue teams to search the moors for his missing son. Clean clothes were provided. It was explained to me that God had in fact answered my prayers too precisely, and that I should not be dissuaded from believing in Him by this unfortunate incident. He had got me to the toilets, which was, after all, what I'd asked Him to do.

Becoming an atheist then would have saved a lot of heartbreak in later years, I suppose. What the experience

Bodily Functions

did leave me with was a subconscious vision of God as some kind of martinet timekeeper, the kind of person to whom one second past the hour was the same as an hour too late. Either that, or the Supreme Being had the kind of sadistic sense of humour normally found amongst public school bullies. But then, maybe God was really like that.

I revved the orange beast away from Ledaig with relief. Connel Bridge was still single-track, but the disused railway which had once made it nearly impossible for our caravan to cross had been removed. Finally, I wound down the twisting hill into Oban, and found myself in hell.

Words cannot express how horrible Oban is – and it's so unnecessary. Facing a natural harbour, backed on to a huge cliff, it must once have been a pleasant fishing and steamer port. Then the Victorians came, complete with railway, and turned it into an elegant holiday resort, full of substantial houses, big hotels, a promenade and, of course, the fool's cap of what is now officially McCaig's Tower, though I've always known it as McCaig's Folly: the unfinished coliseum above the town which mocks the snarling chaos below.

Still one of Calmac's main steamer ports, with excursions not just to neighbouring Mull, but also to the Western Isles, Oban has become the Blackpool of the southern Highlands. It is still the gateway to the north as well as the islands for many travellers, and it is now, at least in the holiday season, a complete bottleneck. Traffic jams all the streets. The pavements seethe with tourists and locals, for this is a busy administrative and business centre as well. People's heads jerk this and way that, searching for something worth looking at. For Oban is also tacky beyond belief, full of disgusting shops selling Highland dancer dolls, cheap and nasty whisky miniatures and the endless bins of 'SPECIAL! SALE! MILL CLOSURE!' woollens and tweeds.

The beast and I fought through into one of the back streets, hidden behind the Victorian frontages, between the dirty back-cliff and the down-at-heel glitz of the main drag. I chained up the bike opposite a really dreadful-looking pub, and a sight which took me right back to my childhood fears of drink, instilled by dreadful warnings of what happened to families whose fathers spent their wage-packets on boozing.

Outside the pub stood a little boy of about seven, holding the handles of a push-chair in which another child, a boy of about three, sat with his head on one side, eyes staring at nothing. Occasionally the older boy would move round to the pub's door, push it open a crack and shout 'Dad!' There would be a muffled angry reply, then the boy would return to his post at the push-chair.

I walked out on to the main promenade, which faces the sea. The old pierhead station has been woefully converted into a cheap and nasty plastic Scotrail monstrosity, and a shopping mall was being erected nearby, in the would-be ethnic shape of a series of malting pagodas. It looked quite appalling, and almost entirely unplanned. Meanwhile, cars literally raced along the wide main street, making it all but impossible to cross. I bought a newspaper, and ate, badly, in a self-service cafeteria of massive proportions called MacTavish's Kitchen.

I had planned to stay in Oban, then go to Mull for the day, return and head for Campbeltown. However, time had always been against that idea, and the thought of spending any time at all on Mull, an island so crammed with white settlers from England that it's almost impossible to hear a local accent, did not particularly appeal.

There is a distillery at Tobermory, Mull's capital, and I have to say that the vatted malt currently produced under its name, which includes some single malt Tobermory mixed with other malts, is an extremely pleasant, mild, island whisky. But I decided to abandon any thoughts of travelling there. I would stay in Oban one night, I decided, then head to Campbeltown the next morning.

Bodily Functions

I finished my vegetarian broccoli pie, feeling decidedly peaky, leafed desultorily through the papers, then headed for the Oban distillery, which is slap bang in the middle of the overcrowded town centre, and quite the best thing in the whole place . . .

I walked out of the distillery, re-entering Oban's screaming torrent of cars and pedestrians. Suddenly, on the side of the street nearest the sea, I spied a familiar bearded figure, deerstalker waggling. It was Donald Gillies, recently moved to his native Argyll from Orkney, where my abiding memory was of he and I drinking the night away in the Kirkwall Hotel while outside the biggest riot in Orkney's history took place (the two local discos closed their doors in protest at a licensing court decision, and disappointed punters went predictably crazy, attacking the board chairman's house, overturning police cars and the like). We, of course, didn't notice a thing, but then we are journalists.

. . . I told Donald I was swithering about continuing on to Campbeltown rather than spending any more time in the place, despite the esteemed presence of himself and his family. 'It's a long way on a motorbike,' he said. 'Ninety miles or so.' I continued to swither after saying goodbye to Donald, who had a package to put together for BBC Radio Highland.

It was then that I began to feel a bit strange. Was it the memory of the great toilet disaster of North Ledaig, or some kind of allergy to one of the fifteen different kinds of smoked seafood I'd consumed the previous night at the Crannog? At any rate, my guts were, once more, after twenty-three years, churning like the blades in a mash tun, and I was suddenly in urgent need of a lavatory.

The station. Brand-new and ugly, it was bound to have a toilet, maybe even one of those speak-your-requirements computerised jobs, the ones which wash themselves out after you've left, and sometimes before. I hurried to the railhead. There was nothing. No toilet. *No toilet!* I couldn't believe it. Things were getting desperate, and there wasn't even a pub or hotel handy. I considered prayer, but rejected this option on the grounds of bitter experience. Any prayer would have to be precise in terms of time, and my fevered mind was bound to make some minor error which God would take great delight in punishing. For example, I'd see a sign saying public convenience, run in delight to the decaying portacabin (and this on the Oban seafront) marked Gentlemen, and find the door locked. A small piece of notepaper would have 'out of order' written on it in ballpoint.

And that is exactly what happened.

I almost wept. Next door were the ladies' toilets, and, sweeping decorum aside, I pushed in desperation at the door, which did not have an out-of-order sign attached. It opened. No screaming women fled at the sight of a large, sweating male in leather and boots, as I leapt for one of the cubicles. The toilet pan was smashed. I tried another. There was no toilet seat. It would have to do. I tore off my trousers, and, muscles screaming, avoided disaster by millimetres. I looked up. It was only then I realised I'd left the outside door open, and could clearly see the swarming humanity of Oban passing by outside. None of them appeared to be noticing me.

Fortunately, there was plenty of toilet paper.

I left Oban in a hurry. Perhaps it was only in its vicinity that God played such scatalogical tricks. I was not going to stick around in case it was endemic, and divine revenge extended to other bowel movements. Besides, the toilet had resolutely refused to flush. It was only on closer inspection that I realised to my horror it had been disconnected. Call me paranoid, but as I drove into the blustery afternoon towards the Mull of Kintyre I was sure the Argyll plumbing police were after me.

(from SPIRIT OF ADVENTURE)

Alastair Reid   (b. 1926)

Scotland

It was a day peculiar to this piece of the planet,
when larks rose on long thin strings of singing
and the air shifted with the shimmer of actual angels.
Greenness entered the body. The grasses
shivered with presences and sunlight
stayed like a halo on hair and heather and hills.
Walking into town, I saw in a radiant raincoat,
the woman from the fish-shop. 'What a day it is!'
cried I, like a sunstruck madman
'And what did she have to say for it?'
Her brow grew bleak, her ancestors raged in their graves
as she spoke with their ancient misery!'

'We'll pay for it, we'll pay for it, we'll pay for it.'

James Sinclair   (b. 1952)

Postscript

If all the things I never said
Were told to you when you were dead
You would have lived a few more years
Completely deaf and bored to tears.

Notes on the Editors

Susie Maguire is an actor and writer. Throughout the 1980s she appeared widely on television as comedian, presenter and chat-show host, and on stage at *The Comedy Store* and other cradles of the stand-up performer. She overcame severe writer's block in 1991 when her first story, 'Gift Horse', won a gold Parker pen which she never uses. Since then, many of her short stories have been broadcast including 'The Day I Met Sean Connery' which featured in Radio 4's *Pick of the Year* and was published by Polygon in *Scottish Love Stories* (of which she is co-editor) and by Heineman's Language courses, to teach advanced colloquial English. She is currently embroidering a cushion with the family motto – 'Not Today, Not Tomorrow, But Some Time Soon . . .'.

David Jackson Young was born in Edinburgh. At Oxford he studied Classics and – in the days when student revues were still fashionable – appeared in the show that became the comedy series *Radio Active*. After a few years as a writer-performer in the terrible world of 'professional comedy' (Perrier shortlist one month, penury the next) he became a features producer with BBC Radio in Edinburgh, making mainly quite serious programmes but occasionally indulging in idiosyncratic romps with the likes of Forbes Masson and Alan Cumming. He currently works on Radio 4's *Short Story* and Radio Scotland's book-at-lunchtime strand, *Storyline*. He also writes book reviews for *Scotland on Sunday*.

Acknowledgements

Thanks are due to the following copyright holders for permission to reproduce the material in this anthology.

While every effort has been made to trace copyright holders, this has not always been possible and the Publishers will be glad to make good any omissions in future editions.

STORIES AND LONGER PIECES

IAN PATTISON: to the author for 'Rab's First Rant'.
TOM MORTON: to Mainstream Publishers for 'Bodily Functions', from *Spirit of Adventure*, 1992.
ELSPETH DAVIE to Sheil Land Associates Ltd on behalf of the estate of Elspeth Davie for 'Allergy', from *Modern Scottish Short Stories*, (ed. Fred Urquhart & Giles Gordon) 1968.
ALASDAIR GRAY: to Bloomsbury Publishers for 'The Trendelenburg Position', from *Ten Tales Tall and True*, 1993.
DAVID DEANS: to the author for 'Stone-Age Sheep' from *The Peatman*, Polygon.
DAVID KILBY: to the author for 'A Tale of Ordinary Love.'
DAVID CROOKS: to the author for 'Spaced Out.'
PATRICIA HANNAH: to the author for 'Congress with Poets'.
LEONARD MAGUIRE: to the author for 'A Literary Football Match'.
SUSIE MAGUIRE: to the author for 'Barry Norman's Tie.'
IRVINE WELSH: to Jonathan Cape Publishers for 'Where the Debris Meets the Sea', from *The Acid House*.
LUDOVIC KENNEDY: to Transworld Publishers Ltd for 'In Bed with an Elephant'.
RAYMOND TRAVERS: for 'In the Dock: Irvine Welsh'; first published by *Scotland on Sunday*.
MURIEL GRAY: to Mainstream Publishers for 'Cutting a Dash' from *The First Fifty – Munro Bagging Without a Beard*.
IAIN CRICHTON SMITH: to Balnain Books for 'The Story of Major Cartwright by Murdo', from *Thoughts of Murdo*, 1993.
JAMES CAMERON: to Harper Collins Publishers Ltd for 'Cover Story' from *Point of Departure*.
ARNOLD BROWN: to Methuen and Reed Consumer Books for 'The Night Class' from *Are you looking at me, Jimmy?*, 1994.
NEIL MACVICAR: to BBC Scotland and the author for 'Christmas on the Croft'. First broadcast on BBC Radio Scotland.

KATE ATKINSON: to Transworld Publishers Ltd for 'Holiday' from *Behind the Scenes at the Museum*, 1995.
HARRY RITCHIE: to Hamish Hamilton and the author for 'Brief Encounter', from *Here We Go: A Summer on the Costa Del Sol*, 1993.
JAMES ROBERTSON: to the author for 'Sympathy For The De'il'.
LEWIS GRASSIC GIBBON: to Penguin Books for 'Prelude: The Unfurrowed Field' from *Sunset Song*.
ANTHONY TROON: to the author for 'The Tattoo Reviewed'.
JOHN MCKAY: for 'The Natural History of Scotland' from *Dead Dad Dog*. To A.P. Watt Ltd on behalf of John McKay.
JAMES MEEK: to the author for 'Something to Be Proud Of' from *Last Orders*, Polygon.
ERIC LINKLATER: to Peters, Fraser and Dunlop for 'A Burial at Sea' from *The Merry Muse*.

POEMS AND SONGS

FORBES MASSON and ALAN CUMMING: to Alan Cumming and ICM for 'Glasgow Song'.
IVOR CUTLER: to Methuen and Reed Consumer Books Ltd for 'Blue Rubber Pants' from *Glasgow Dreamer*.
LIZ LOCHHEAD: to the author for 'Favourite Shade' from *True Confessions and Other Poems*.
ANGELA MCSEVENEY: to the author for 'Changing a Downie Cover' from *Coming Out With It*, Polygon.
ALISON KERMACK: for 'Scott's Porrij' from *Original Prints*.
DONALD GORDON: for 'Wee Jaikie's Sang', from *The Low Road Hame*.
ALASTAIR REID: to Canongate Ltd for 'Scotland', from *Weathering*, 1987.
W.N. HERBERT: to Bloodaxe Books for 'Why the Elgin Marbles must be returned to Elgin', from *Cabaret McGonagall*.
EDWIN MORGAN: to Carcanet Press Limited for 'The Mummy', from *Poems of Thirty Years*, 1982.
ROBERT CRAWFORD: to Chatto and Windus for 'Alba Einstein' from *A Scottish Assembly*.
OOR WULLIE: to D.C. Thompson and Co. Ltd and the *Sunday Post* for 'The Ways and Wiles O' Oor Wullie', adapted from *The Oor Wullie Annual, 1954*.
JAMES SINCLAIR: to the author for 'Postscript'.
CHIC MURRAY: from *The Best Way To Walk* by Andrew Yule; published by Mainstream, thanks for permission for excerpts throughout.